Creatures & Colors

A Magical Coloring Adventure

Belongs To

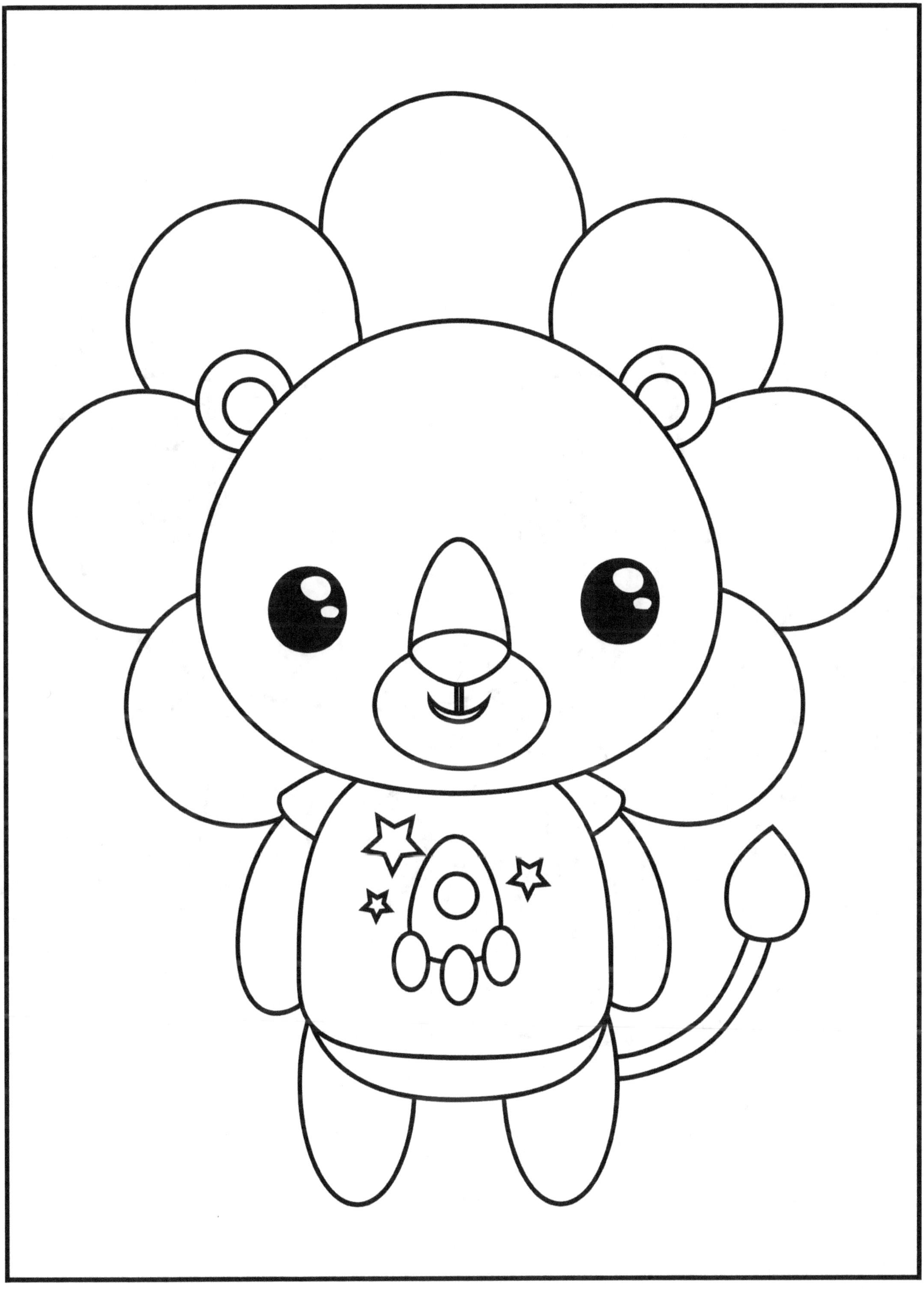

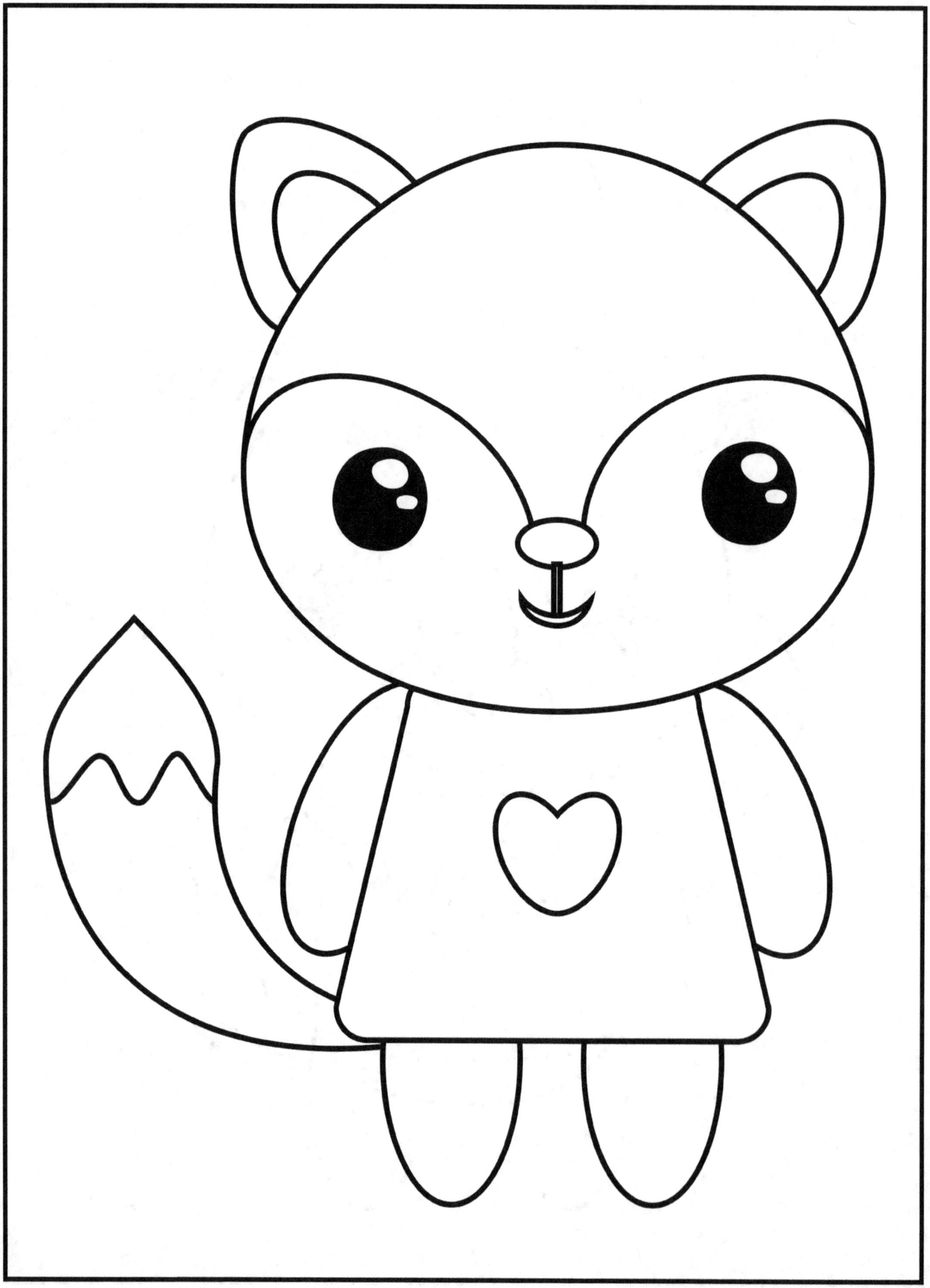

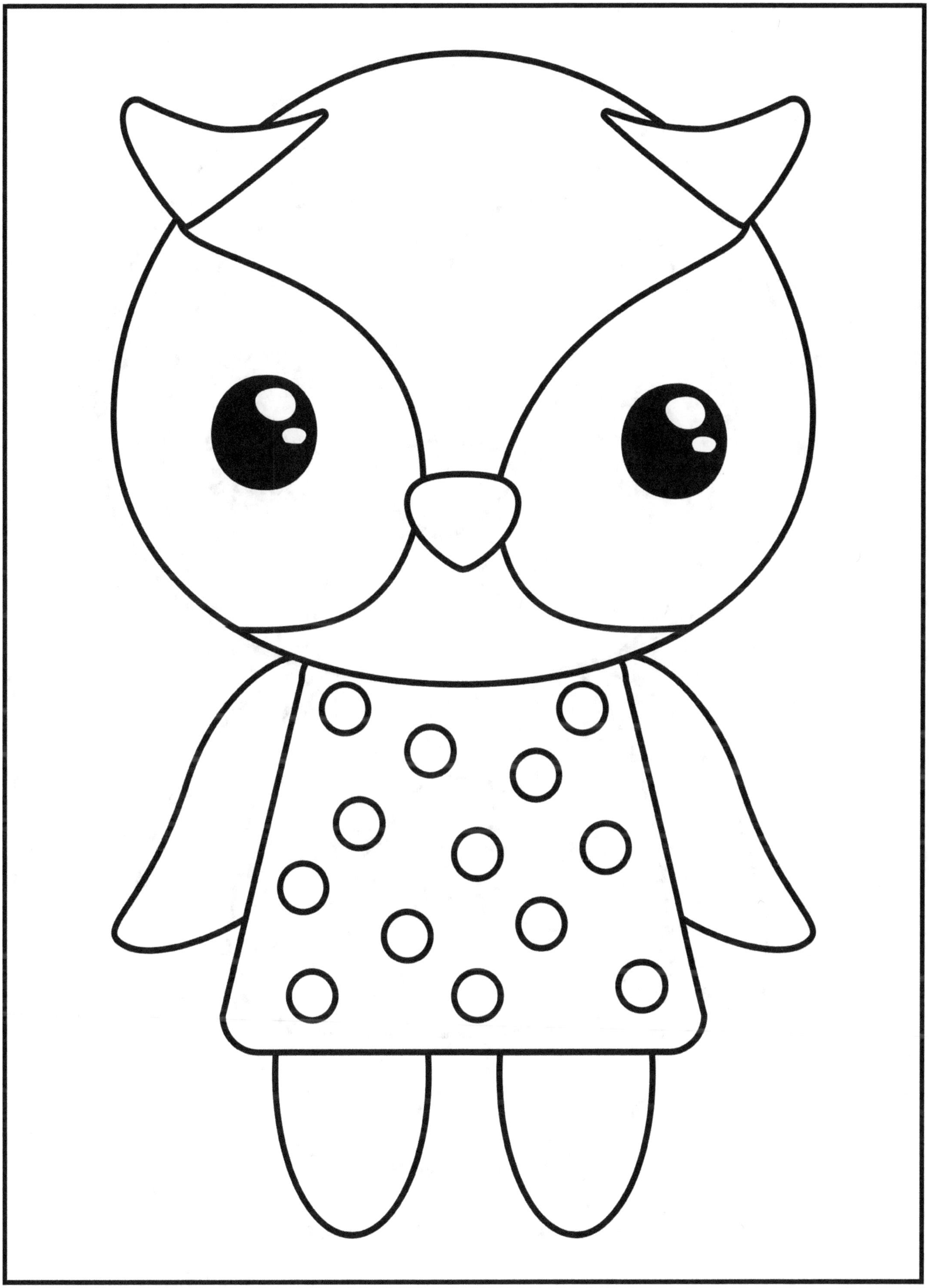

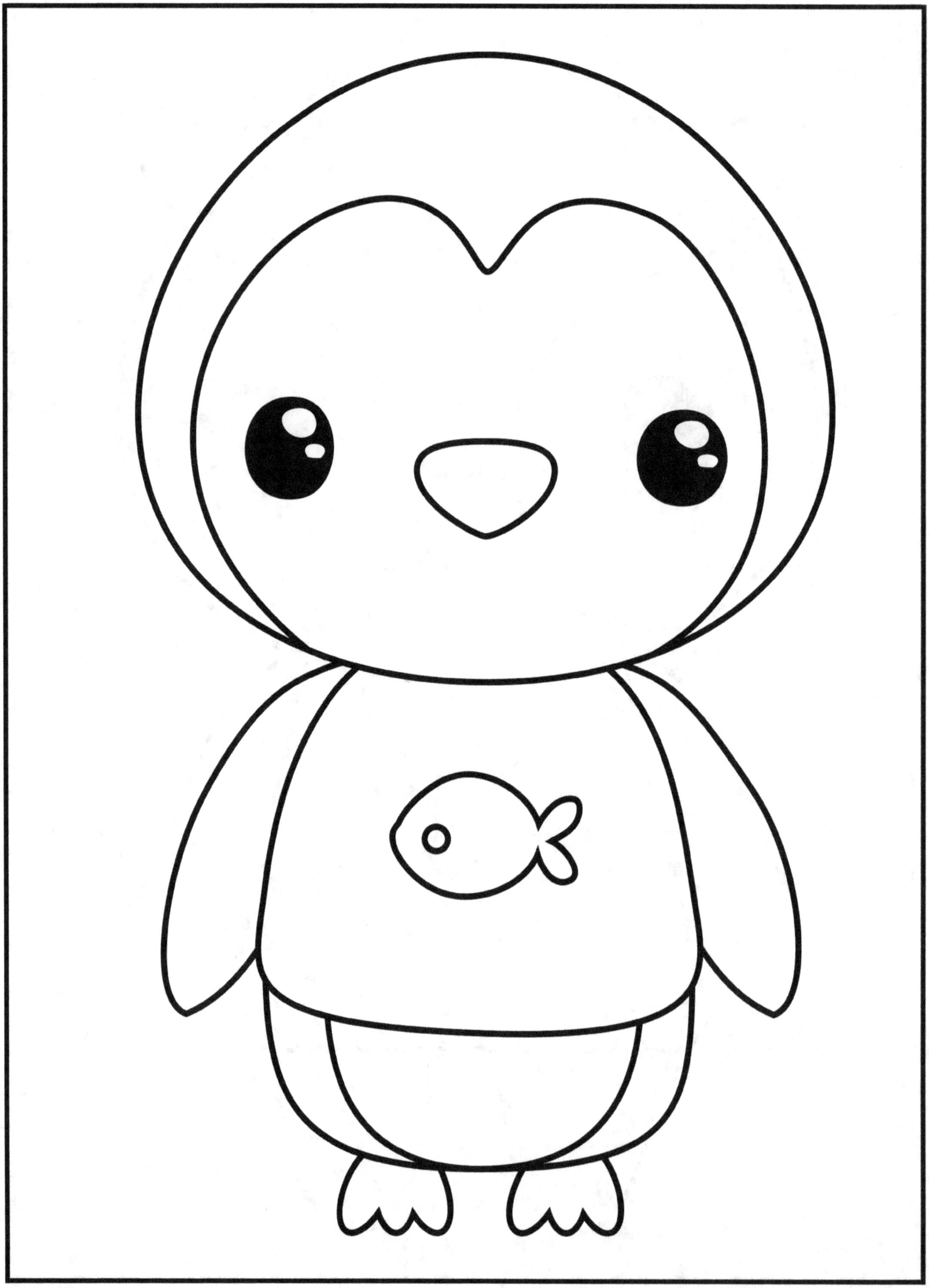

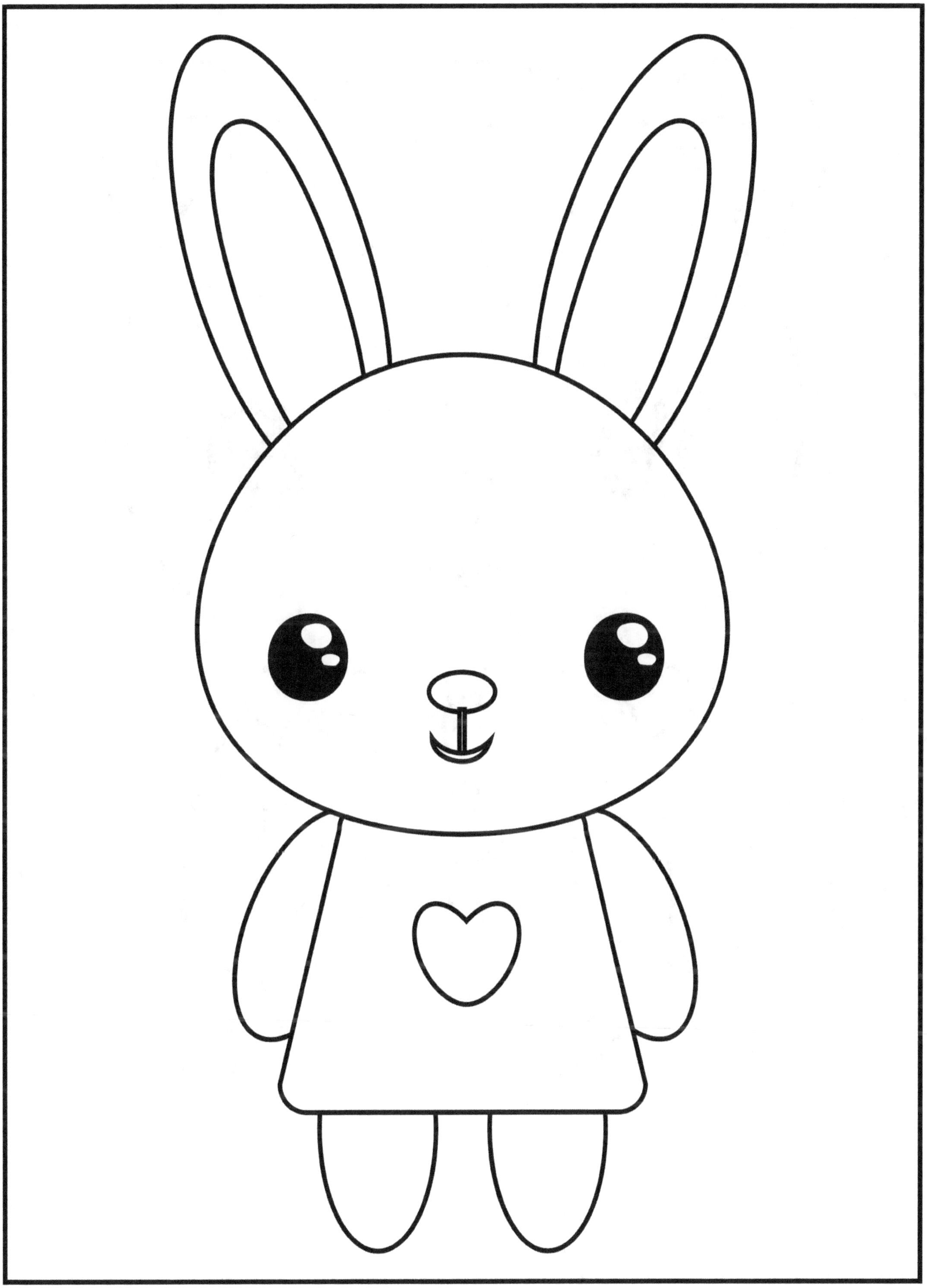

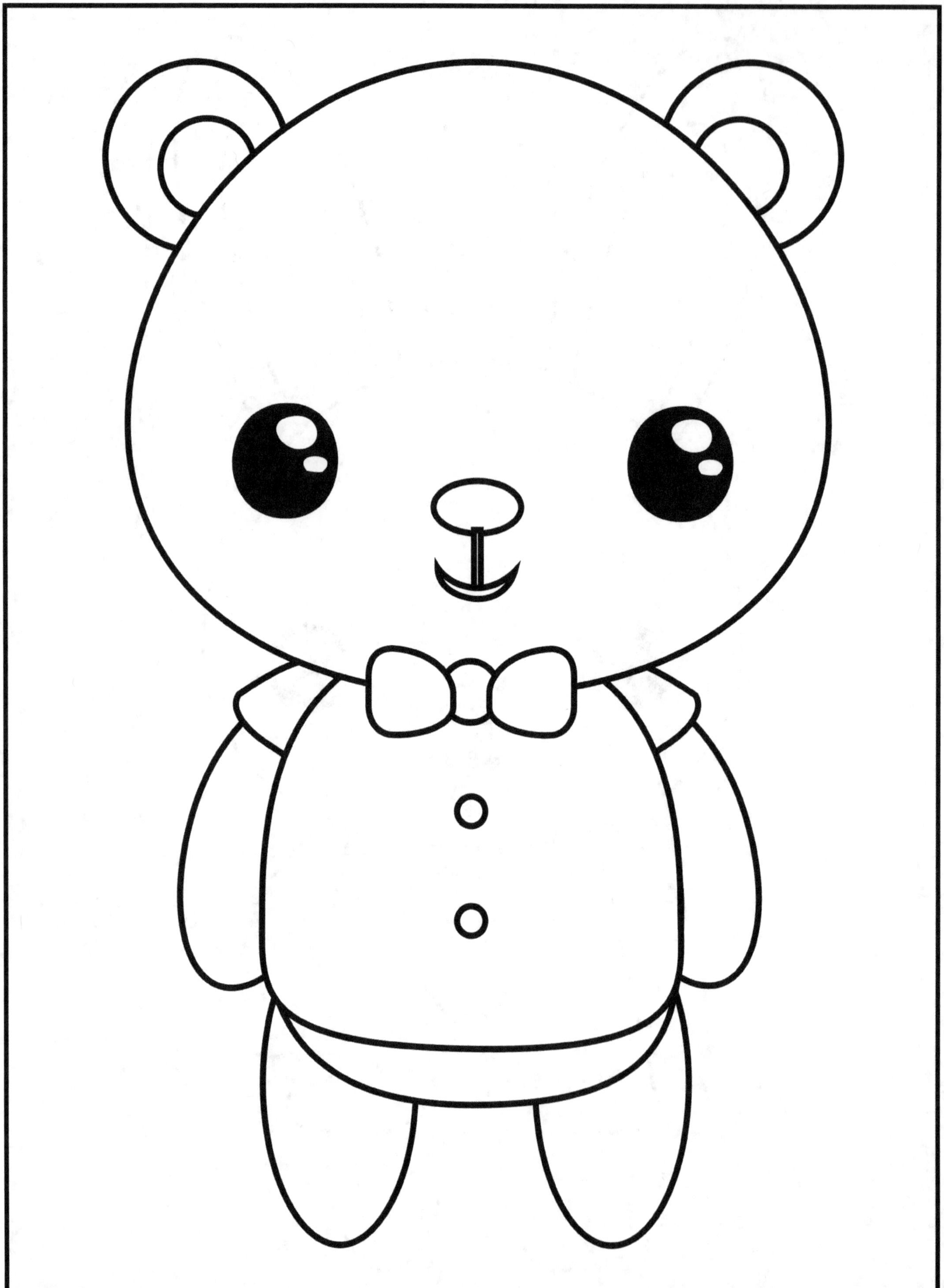

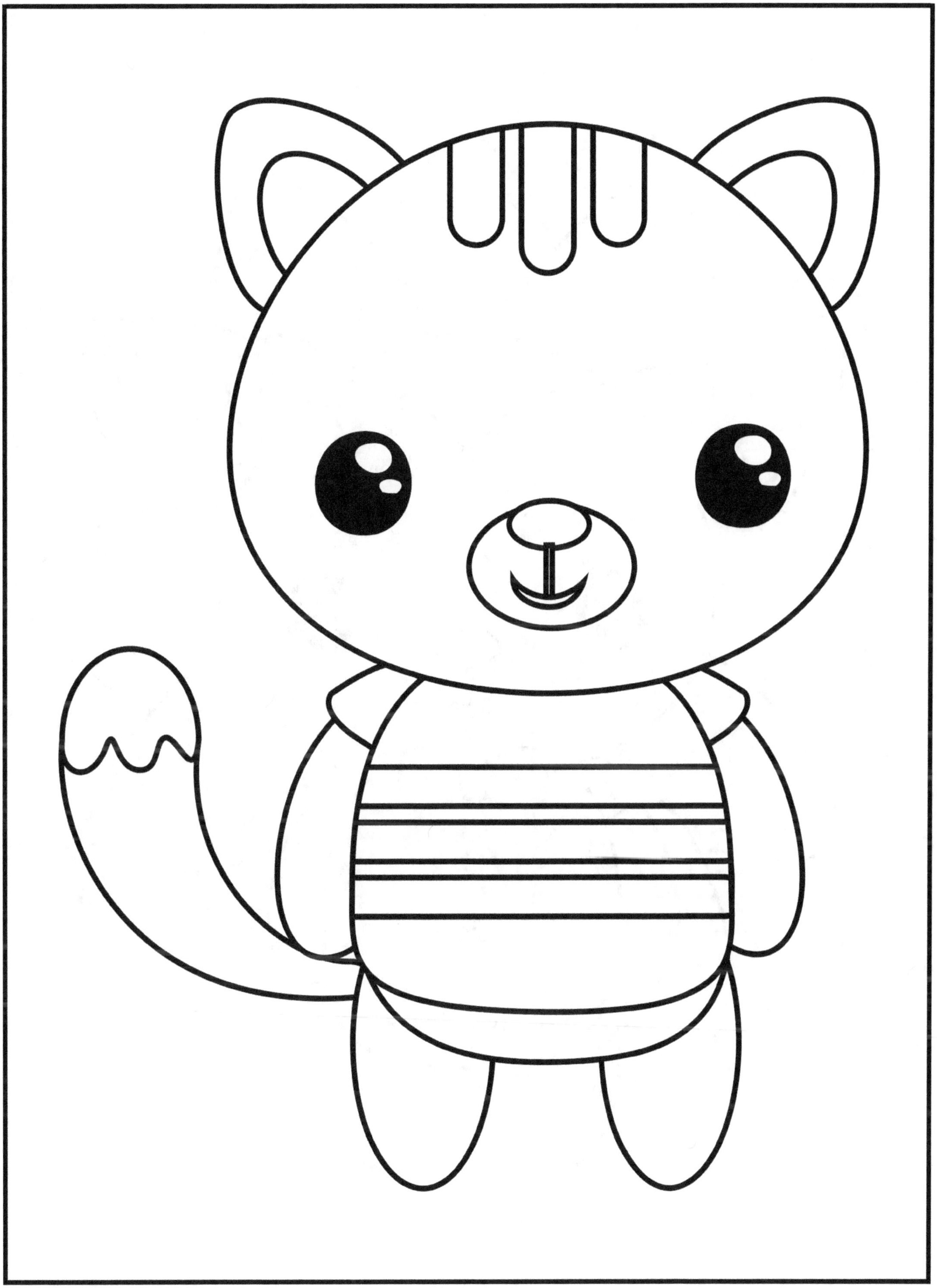

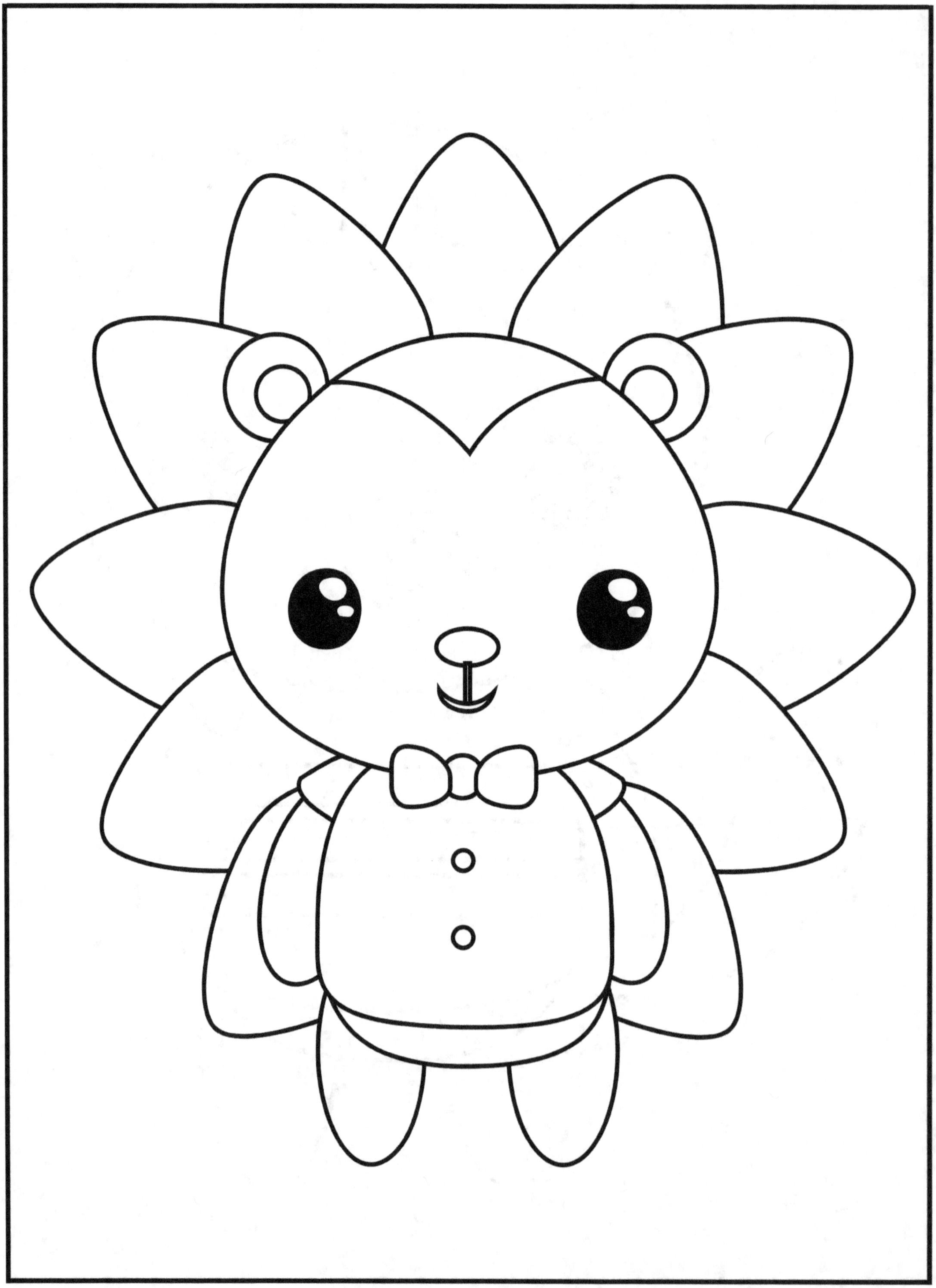

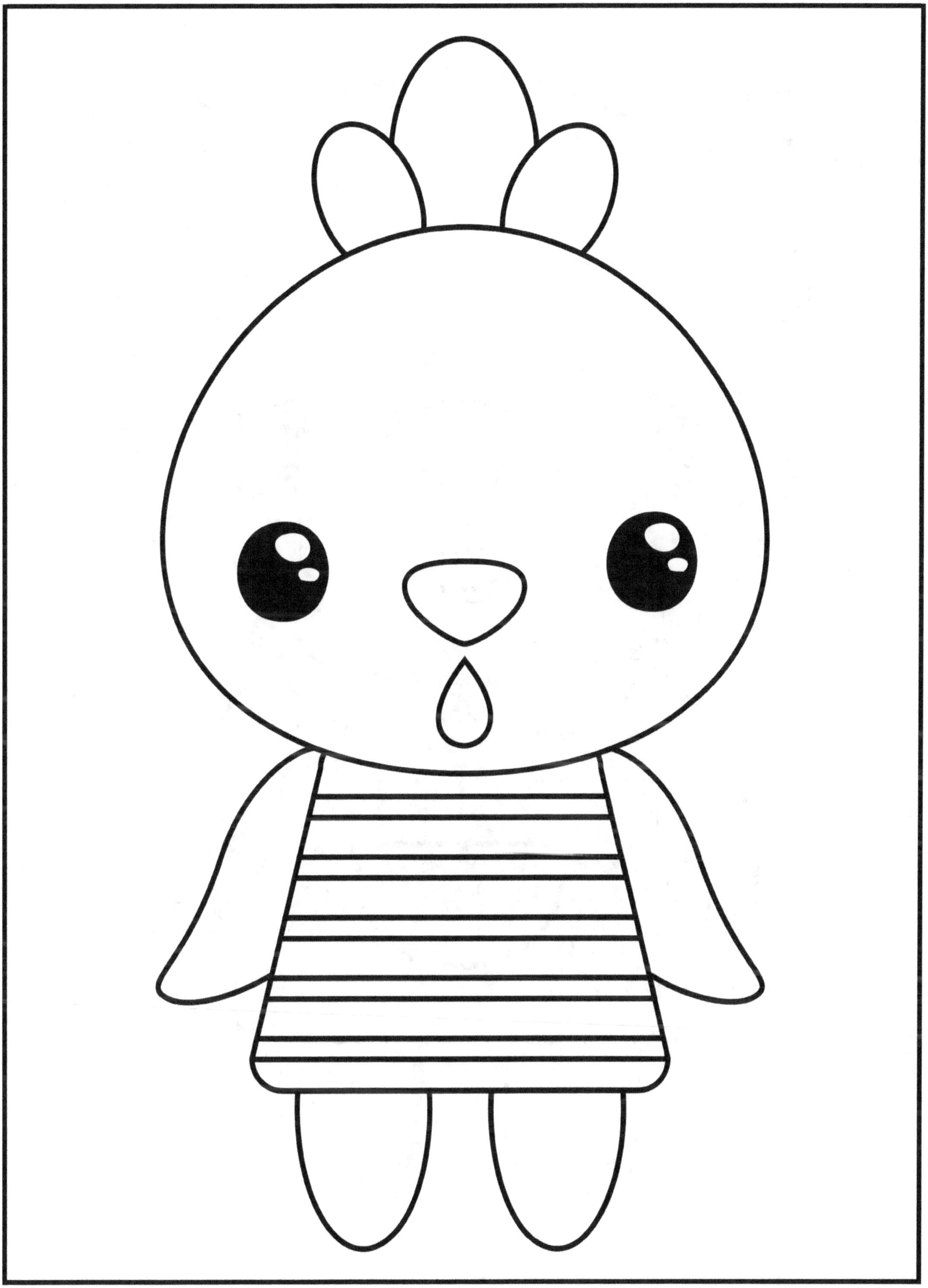

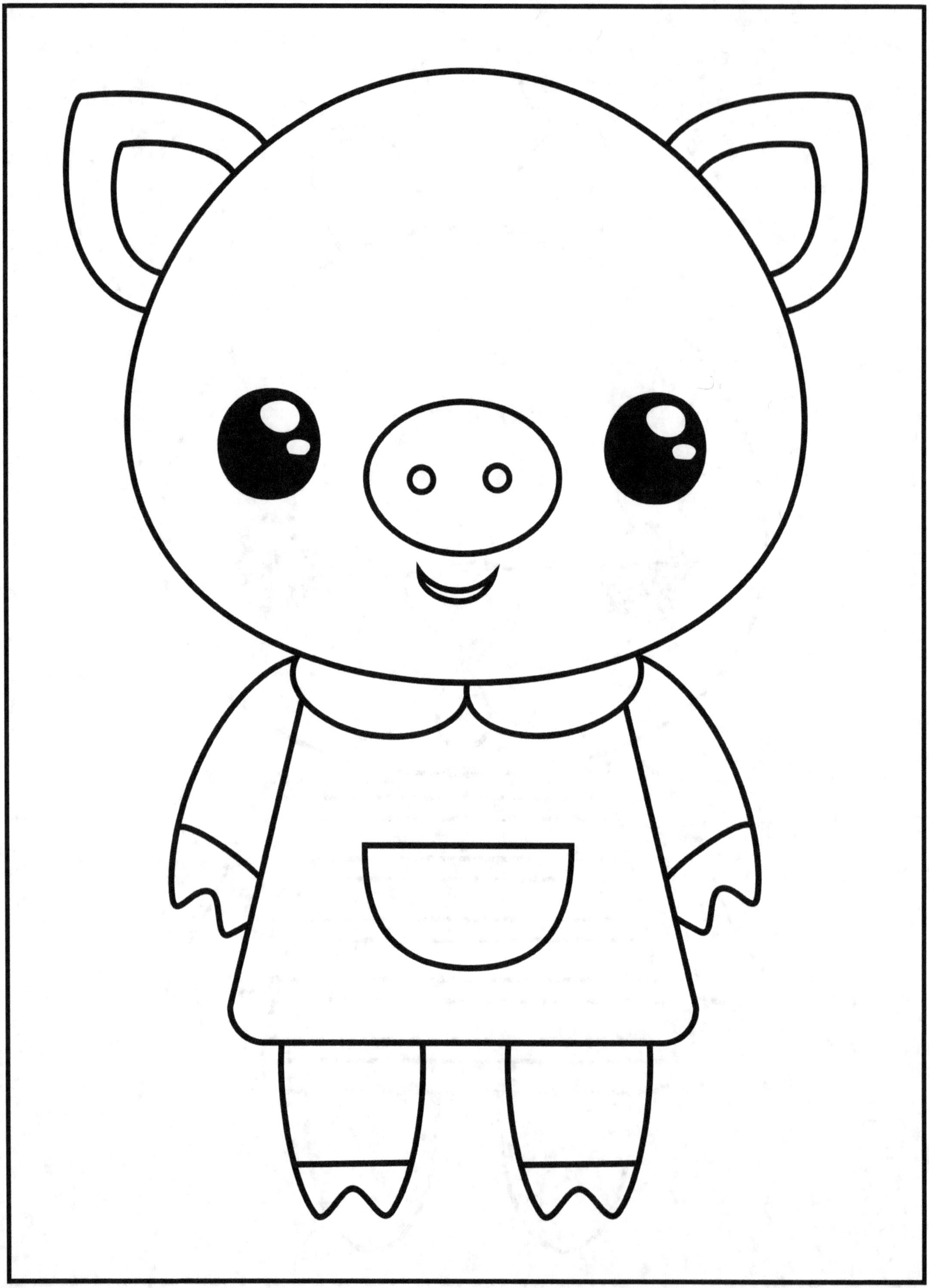

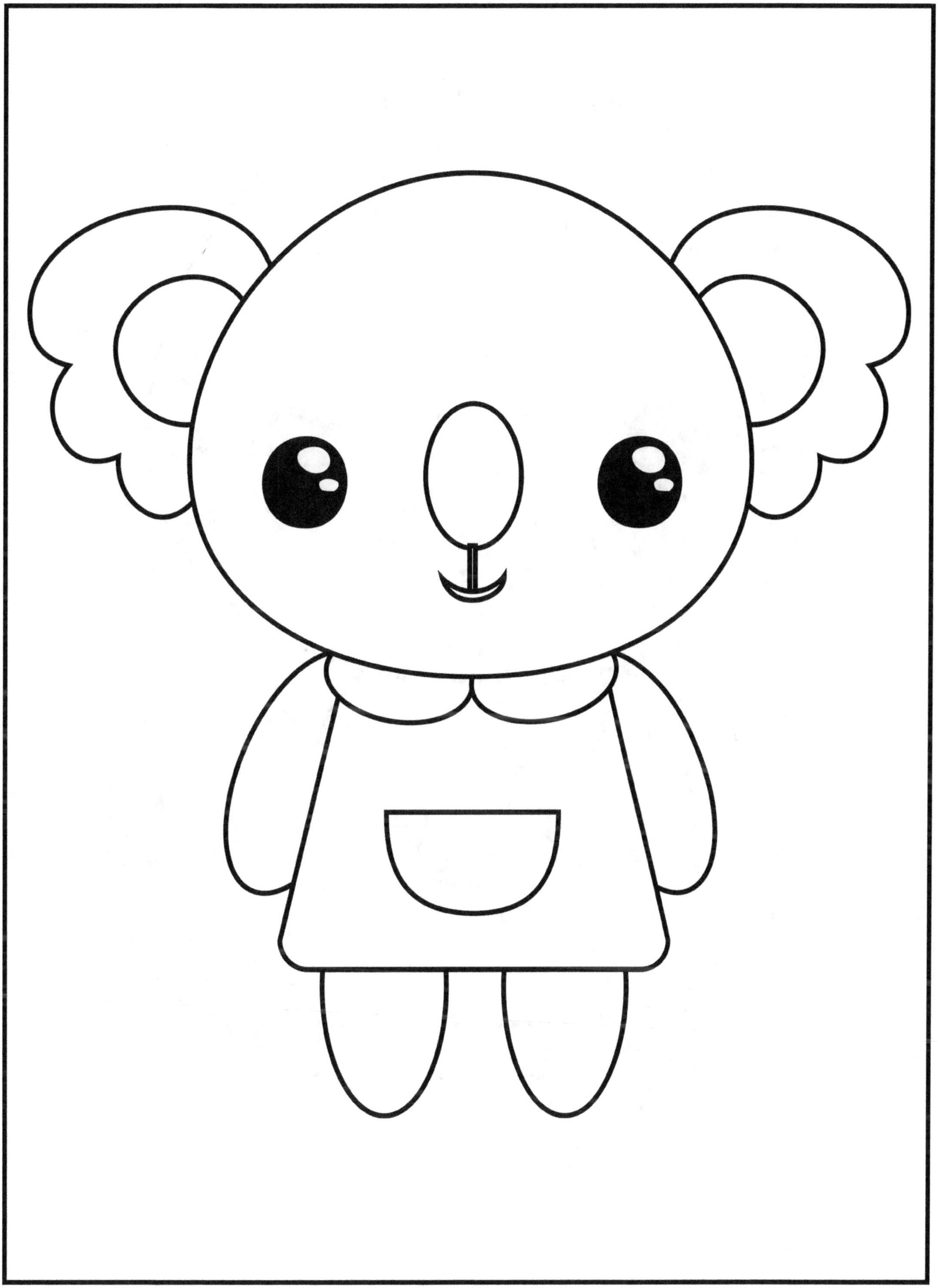

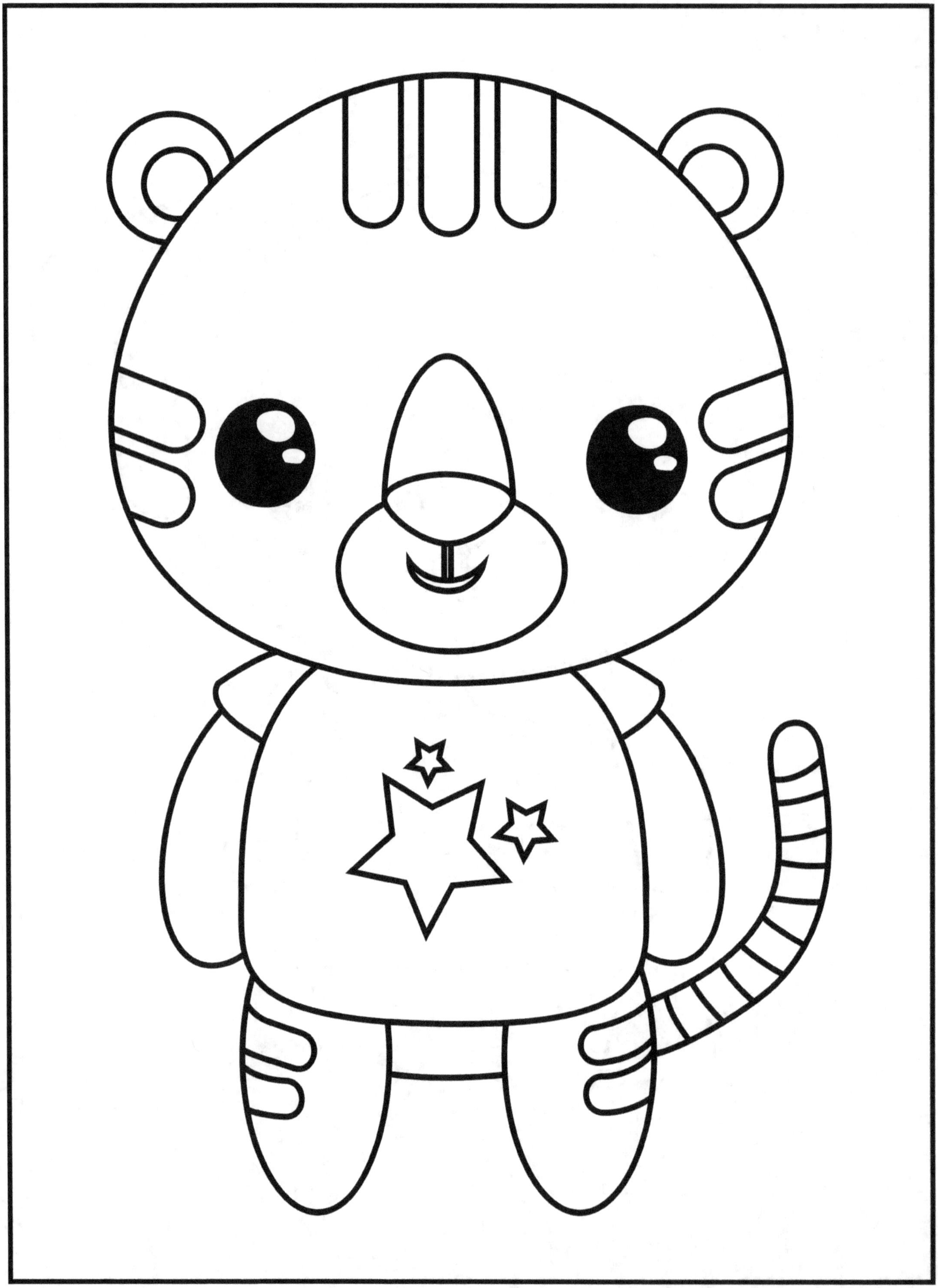

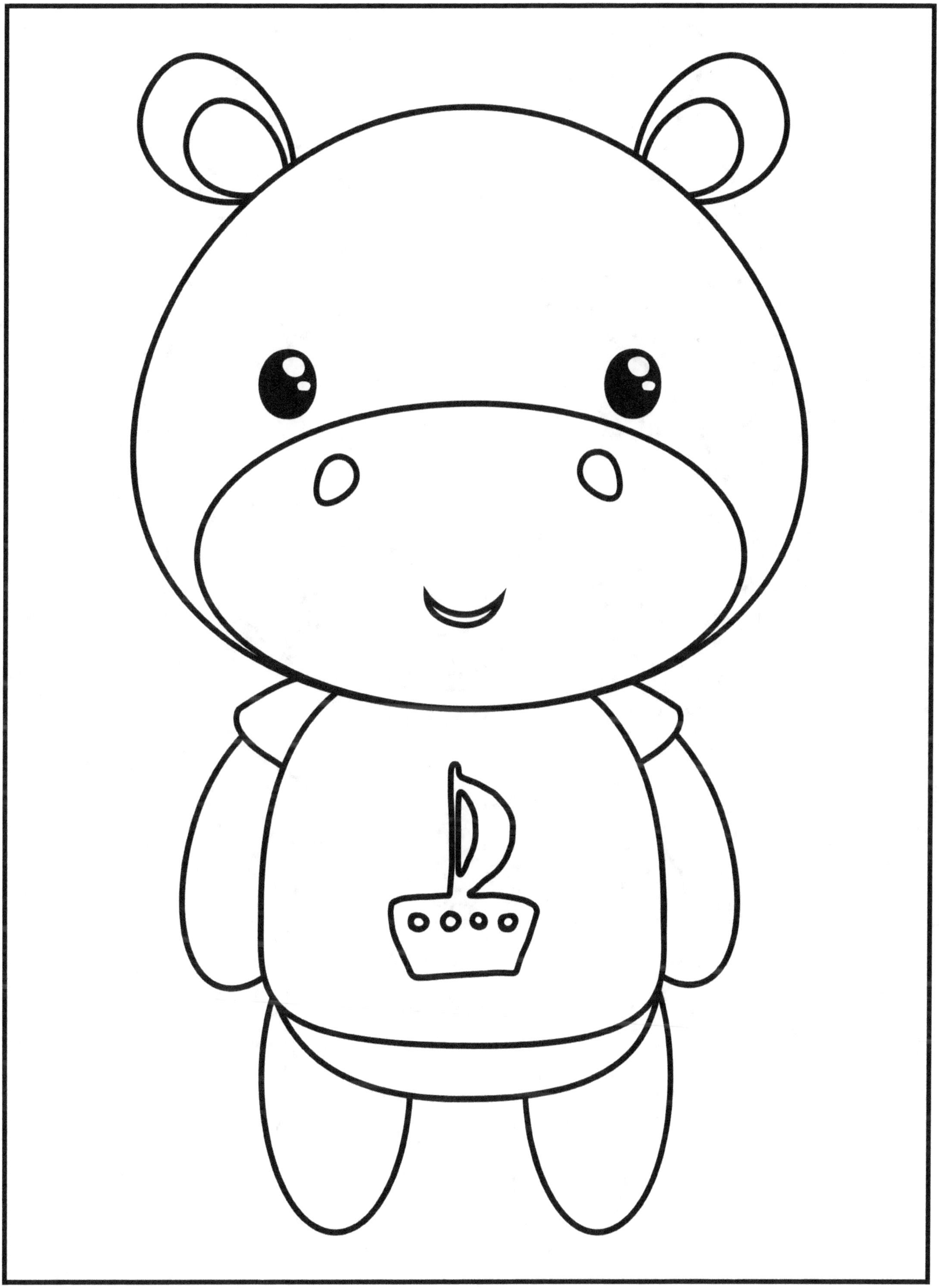

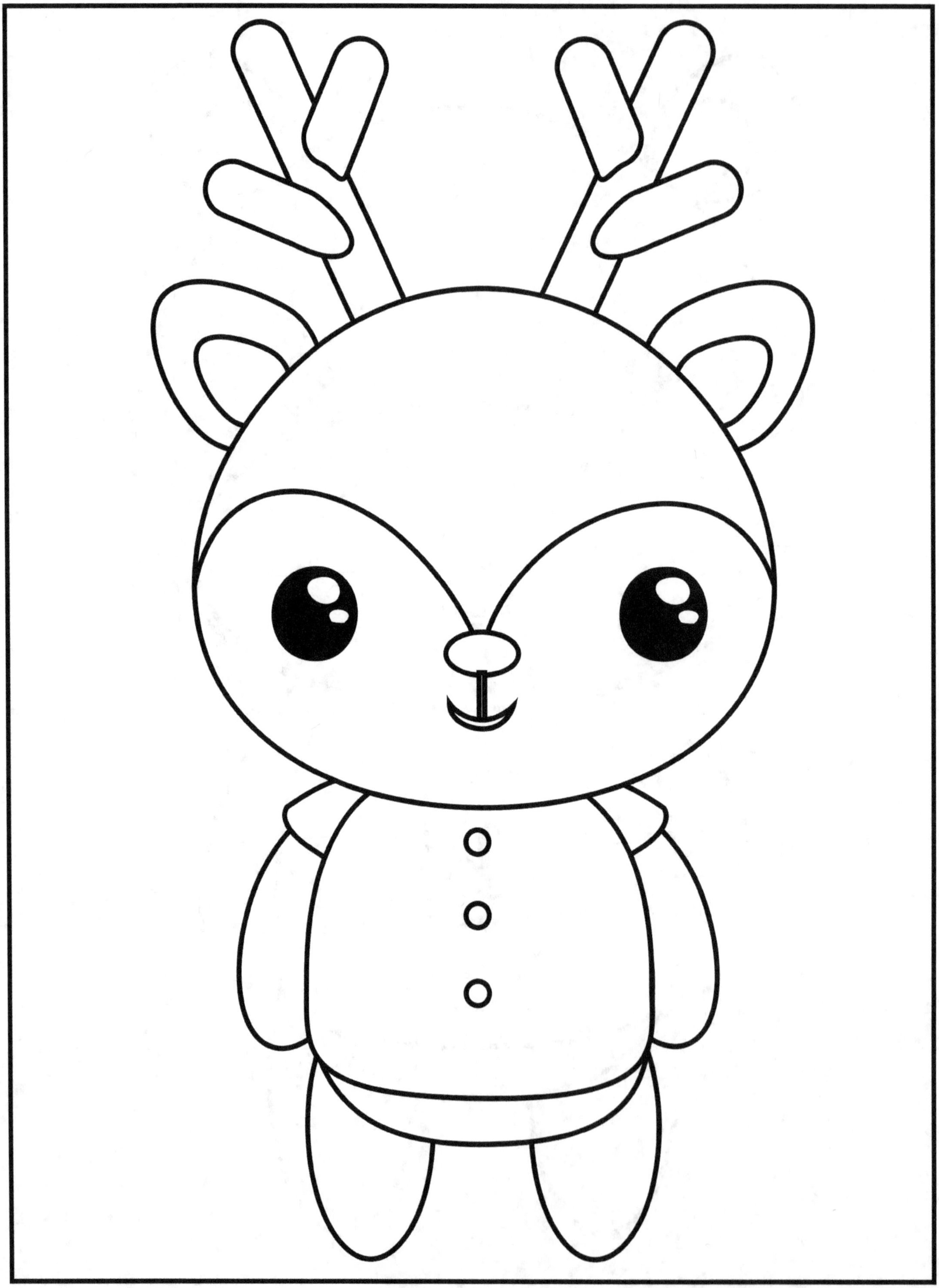

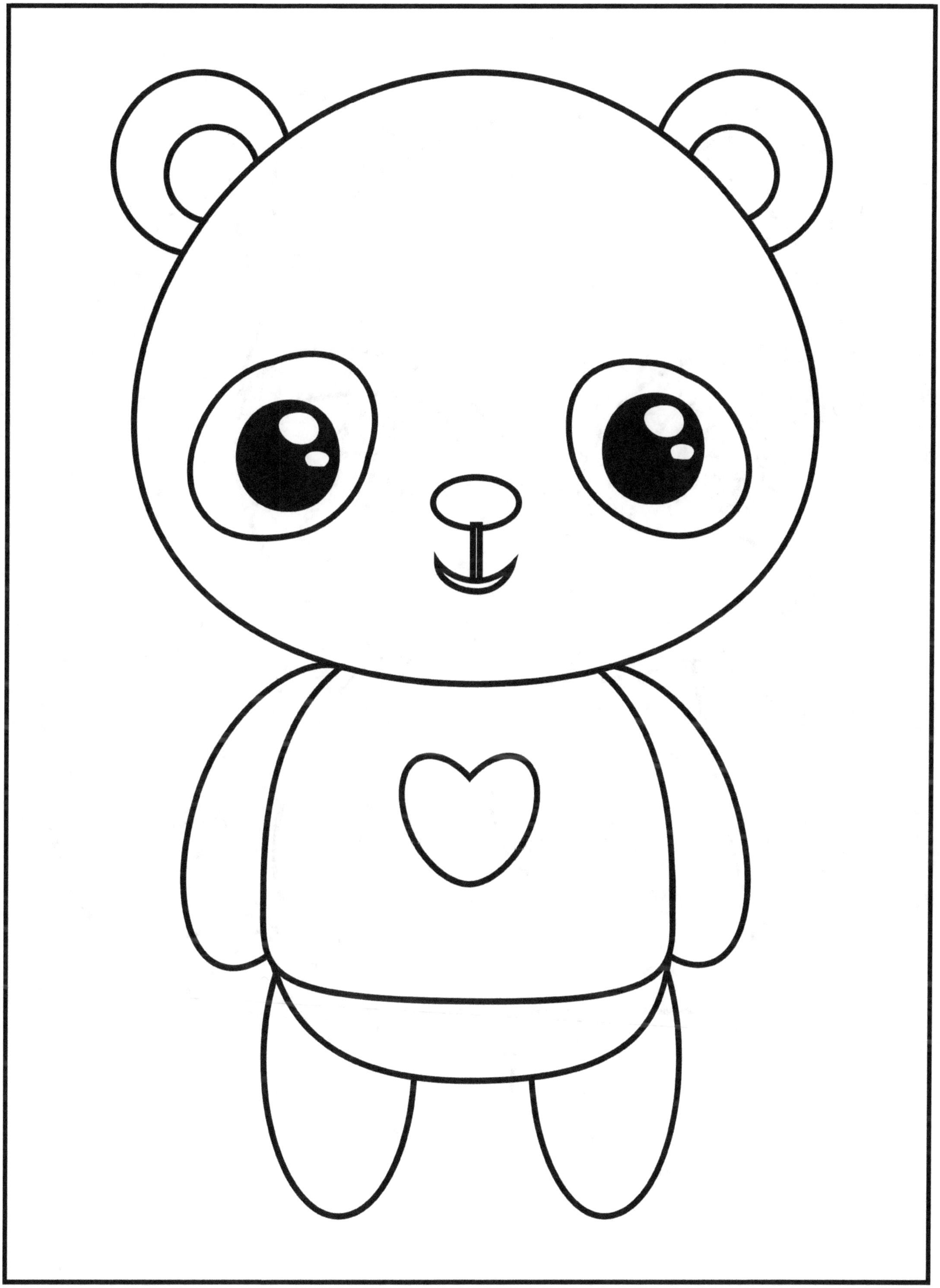

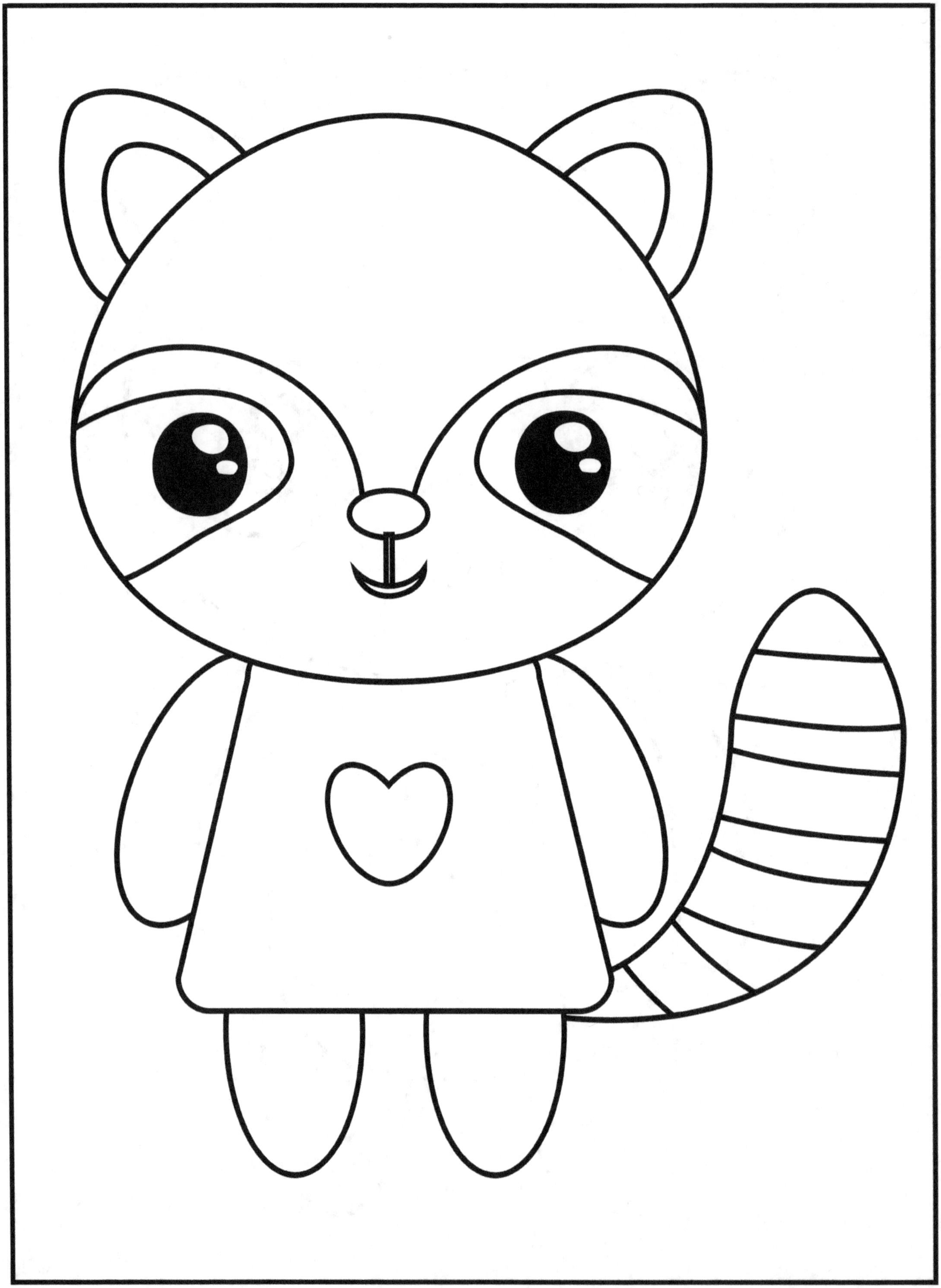

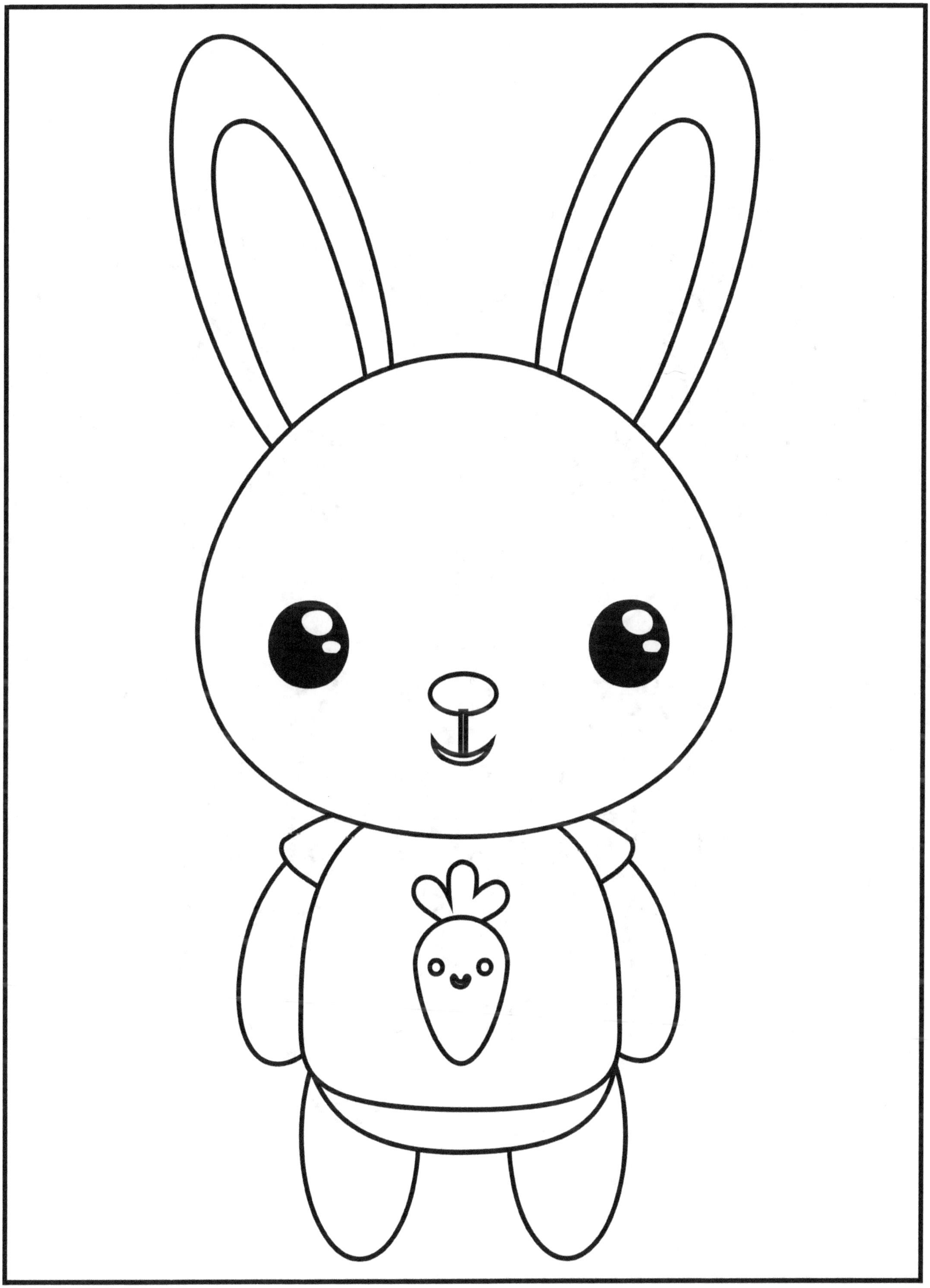

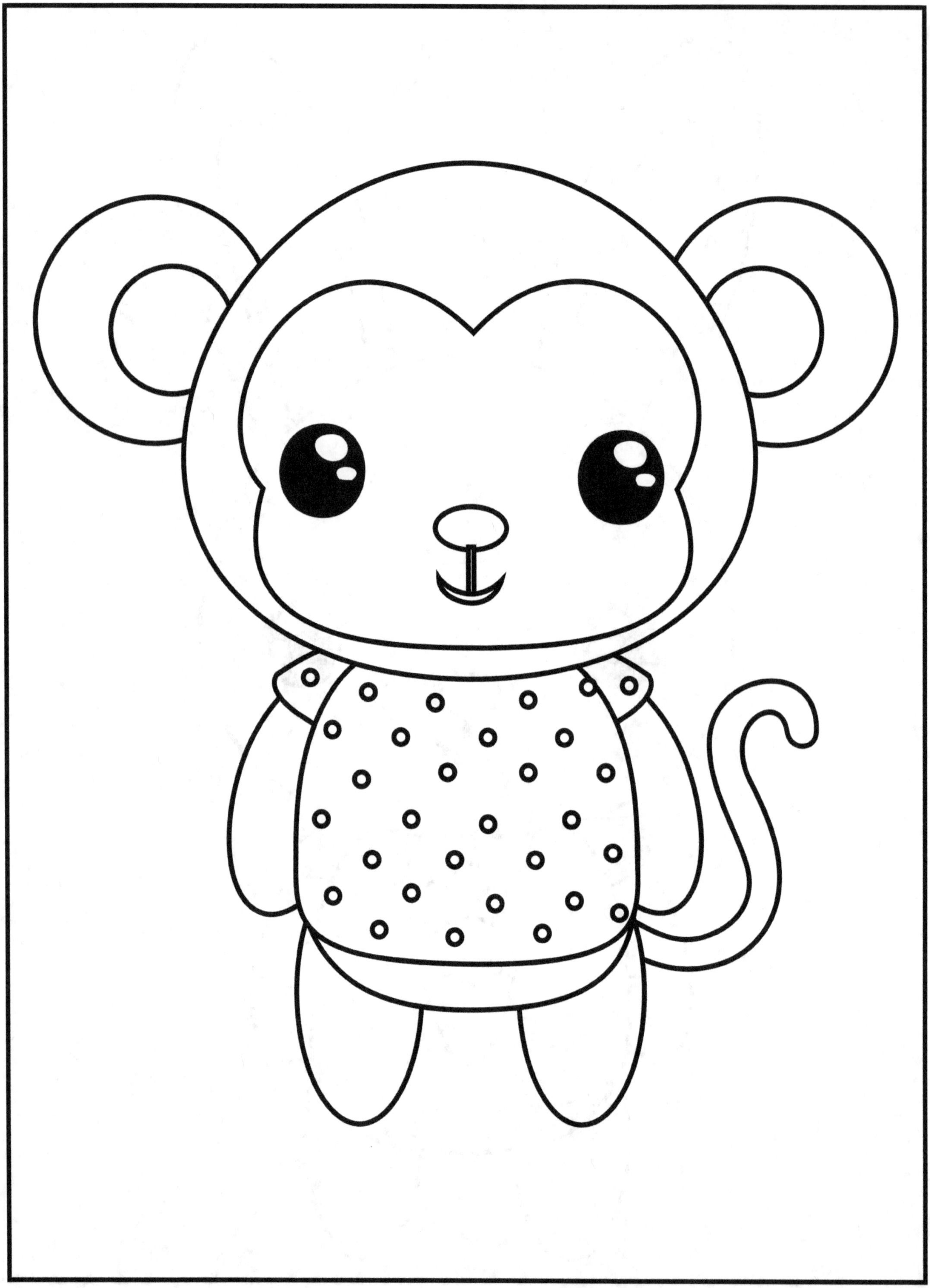

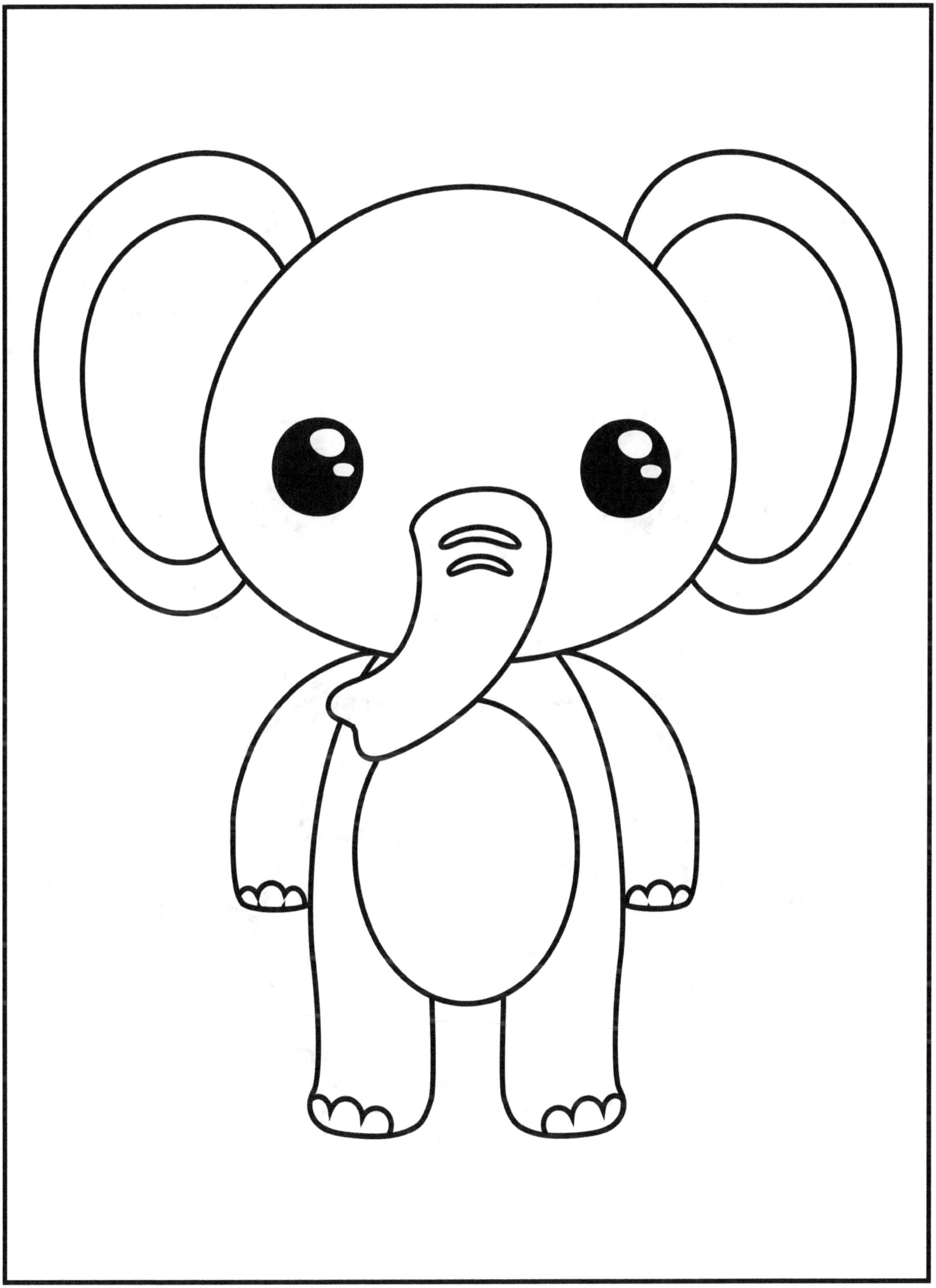

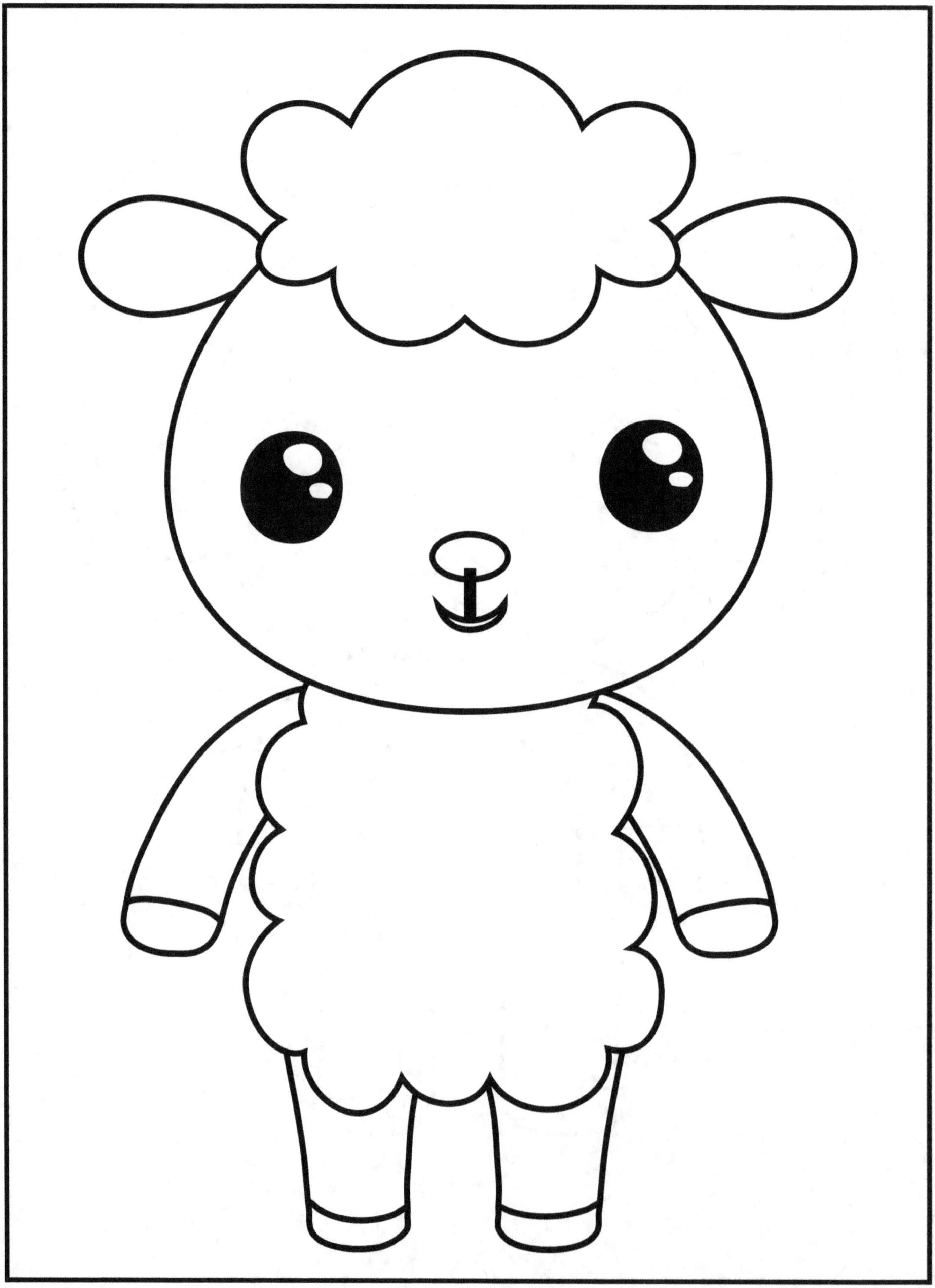

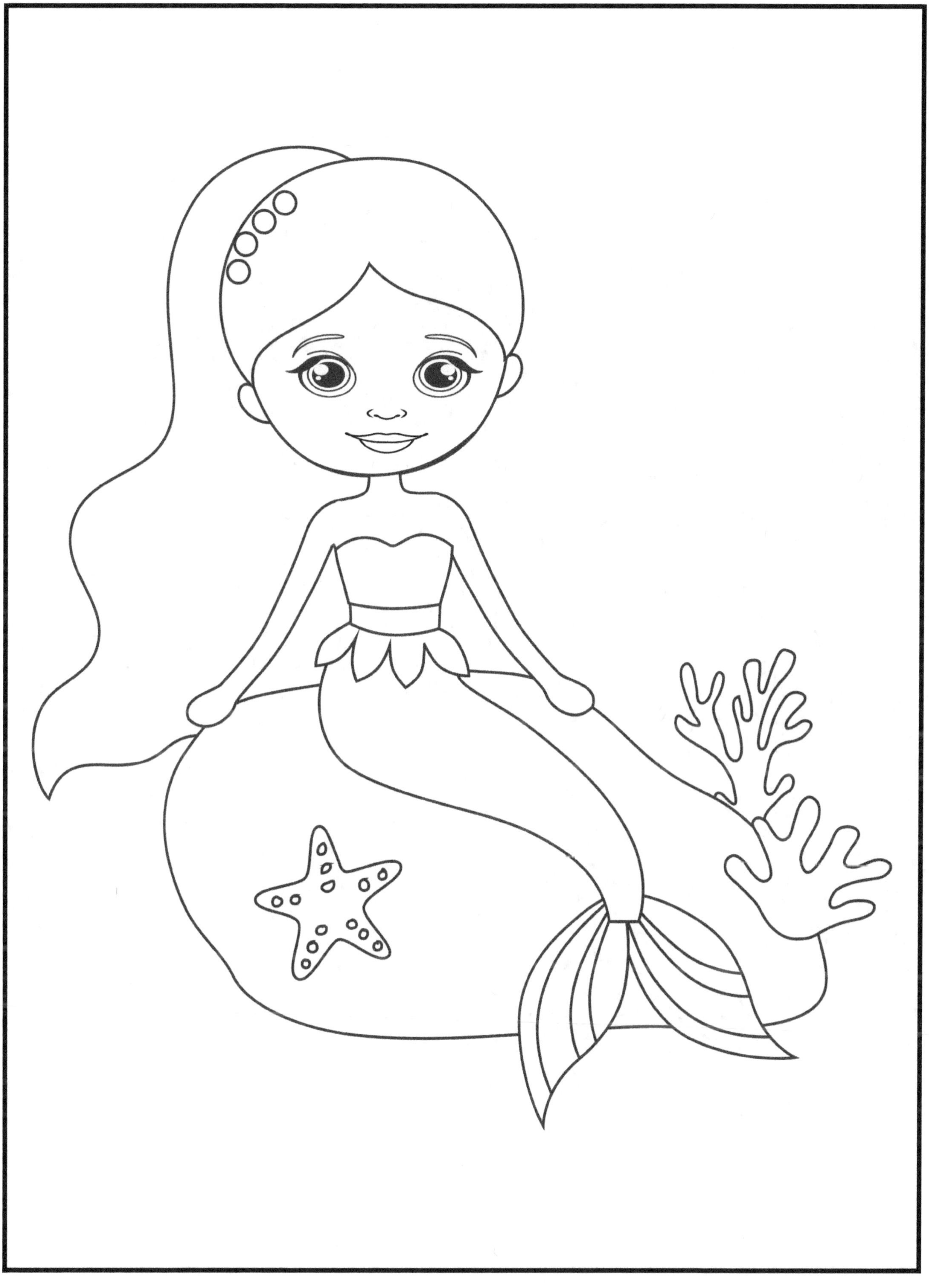

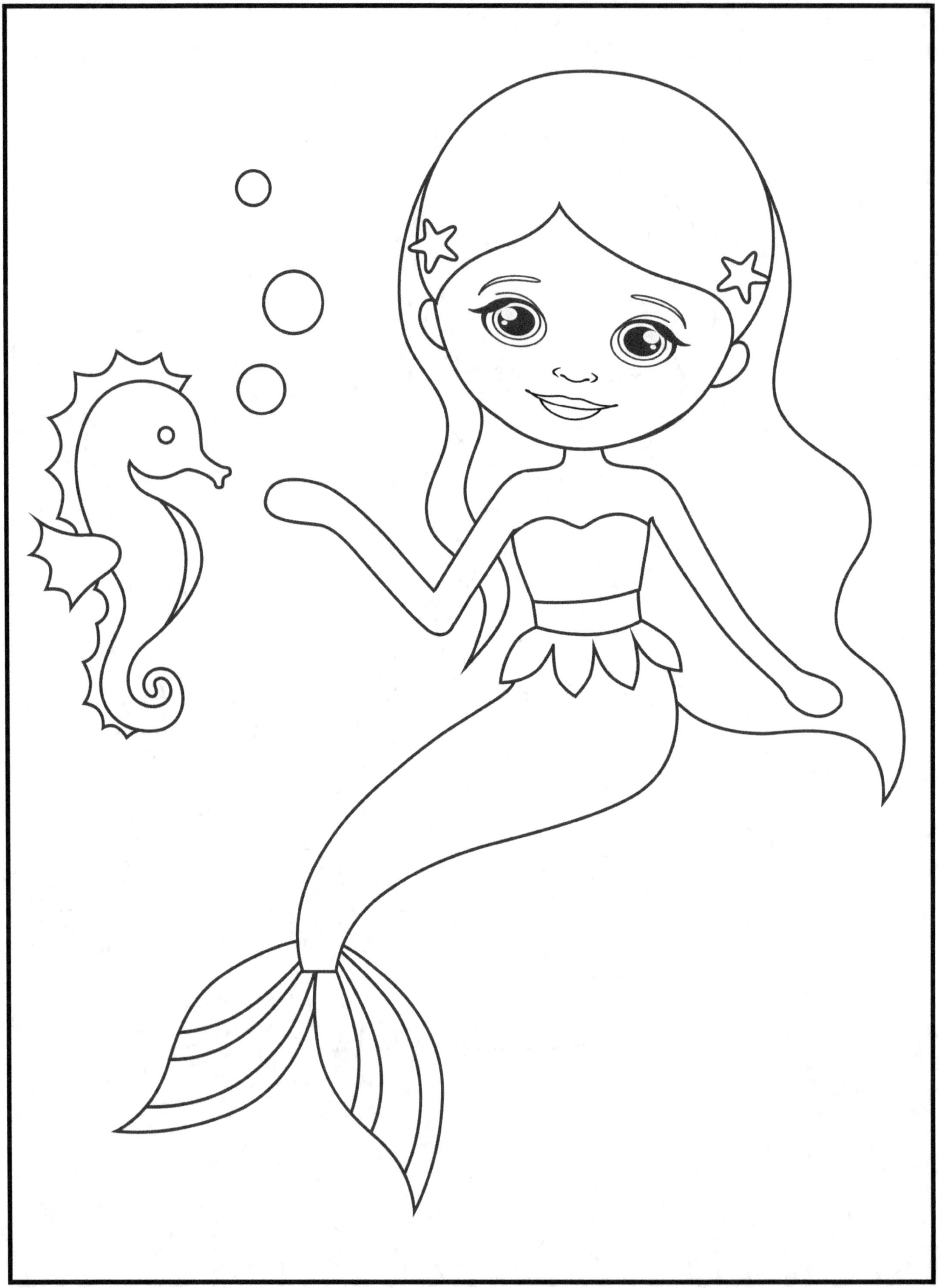

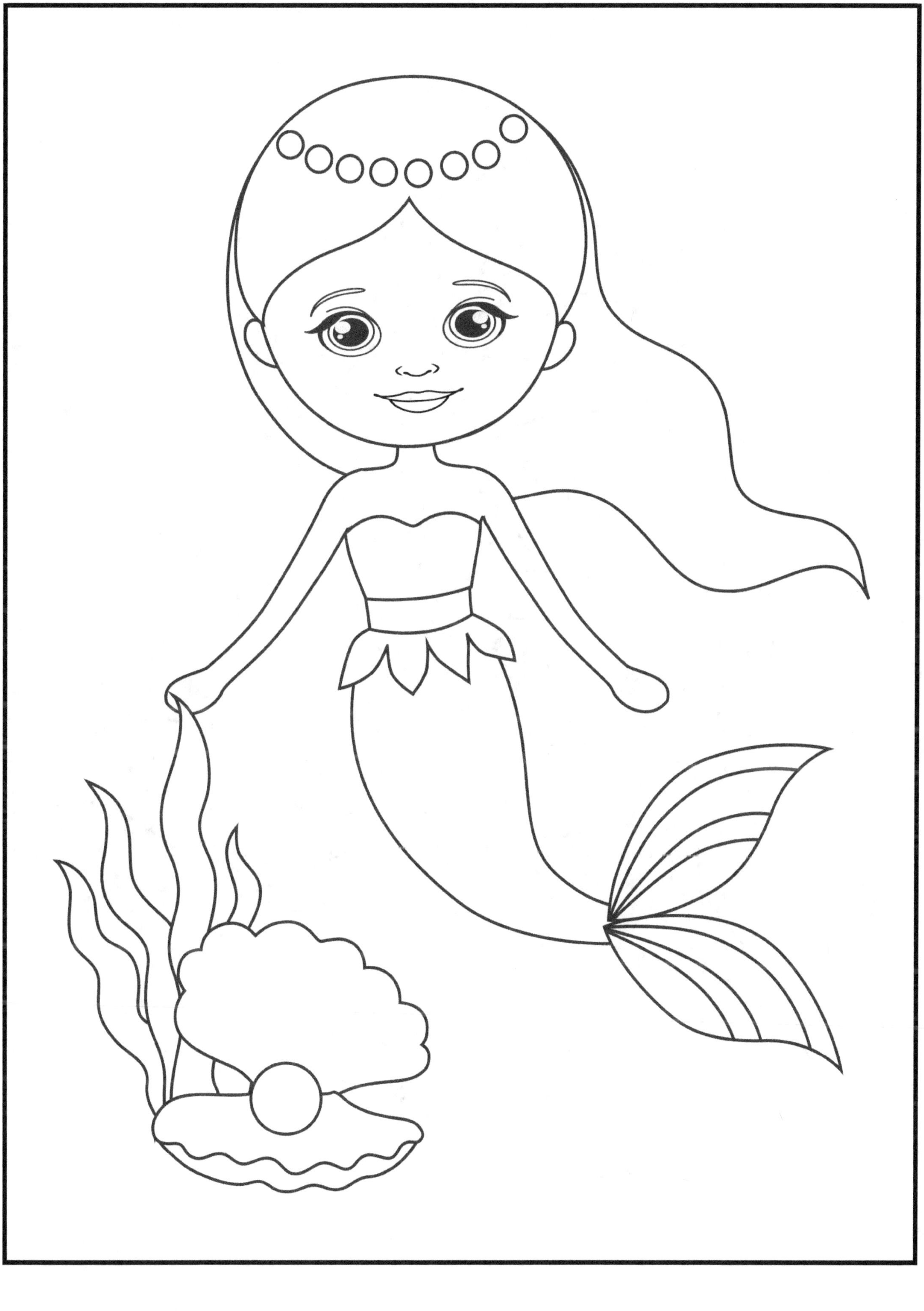

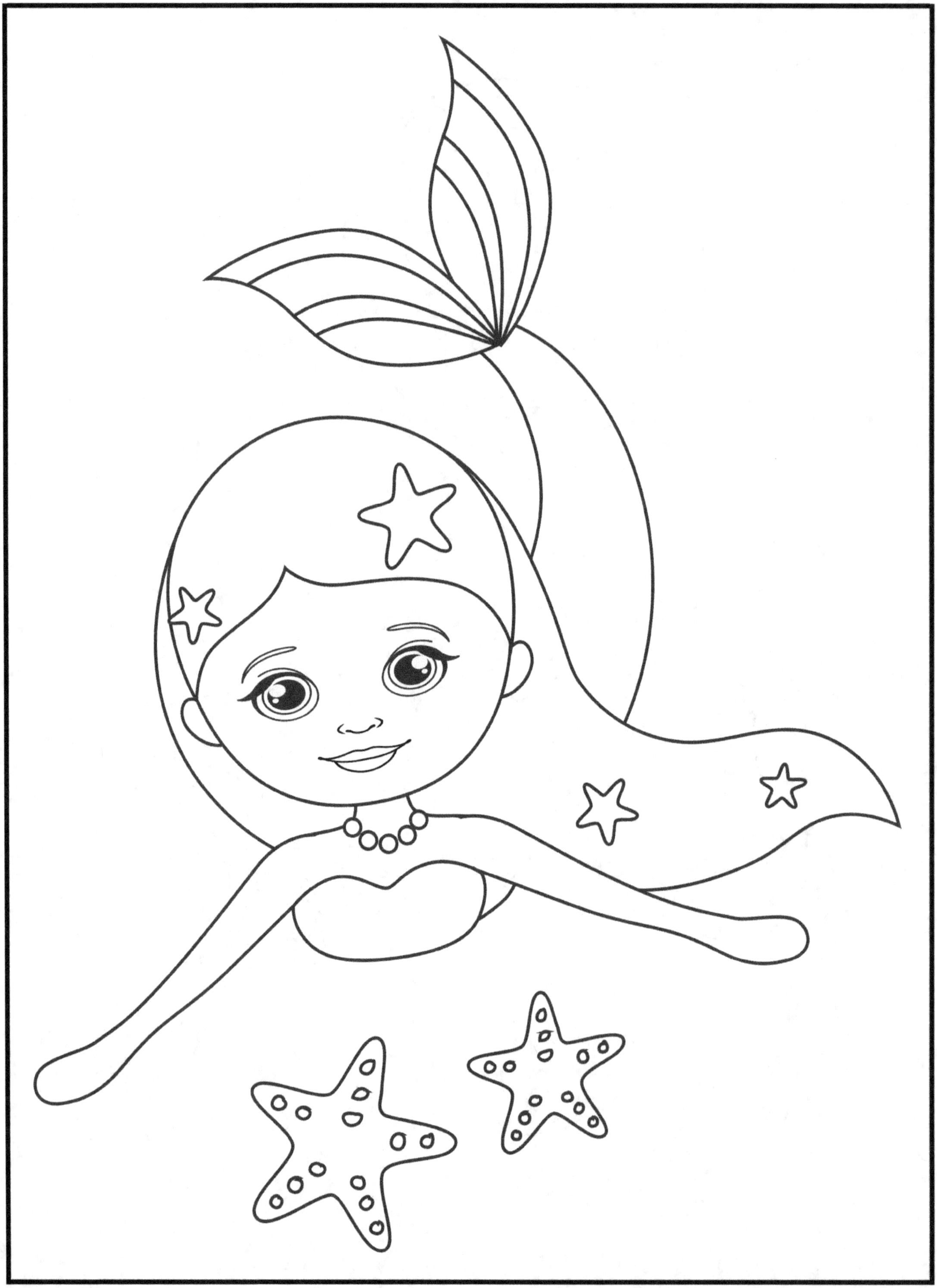

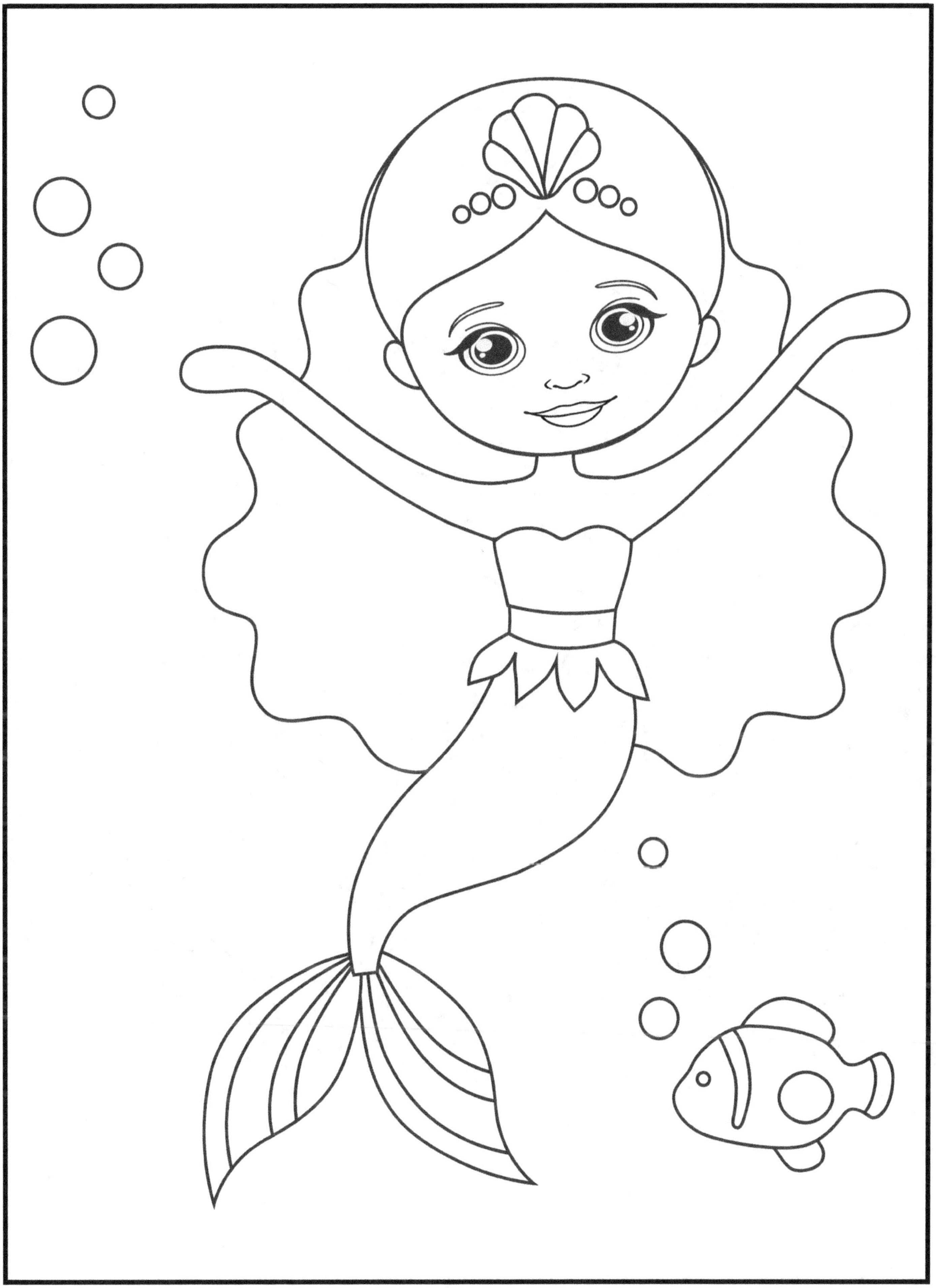

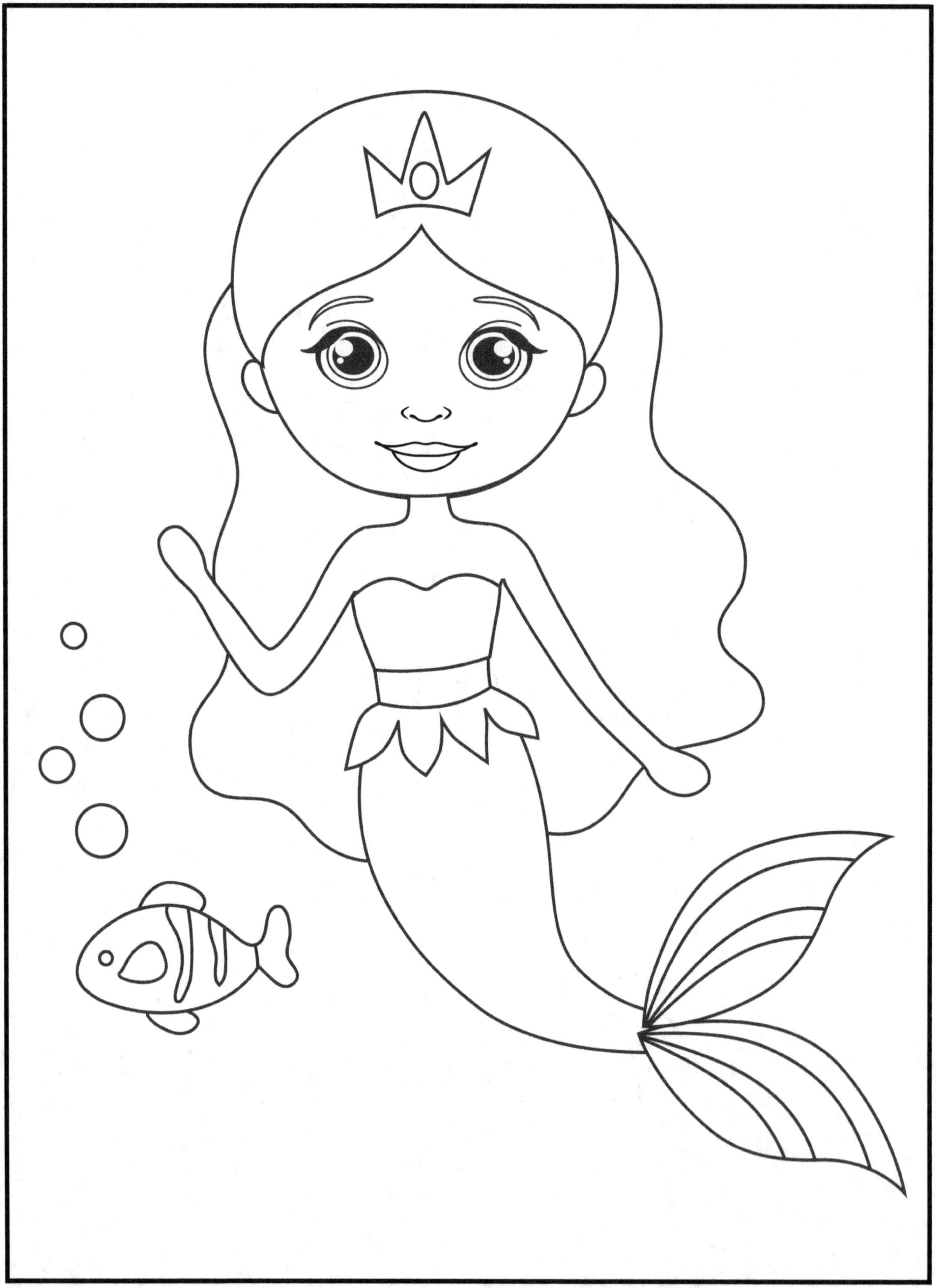

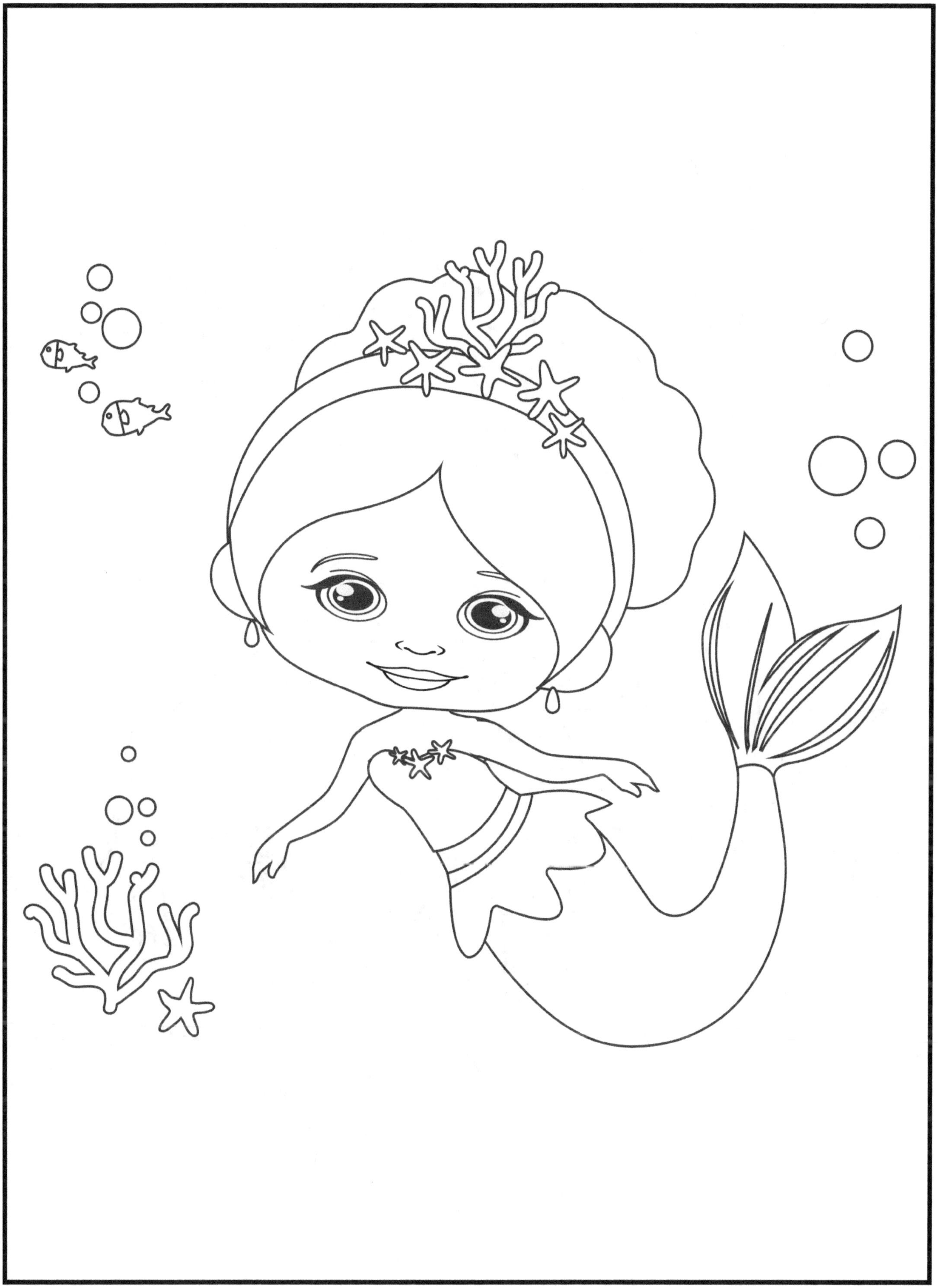

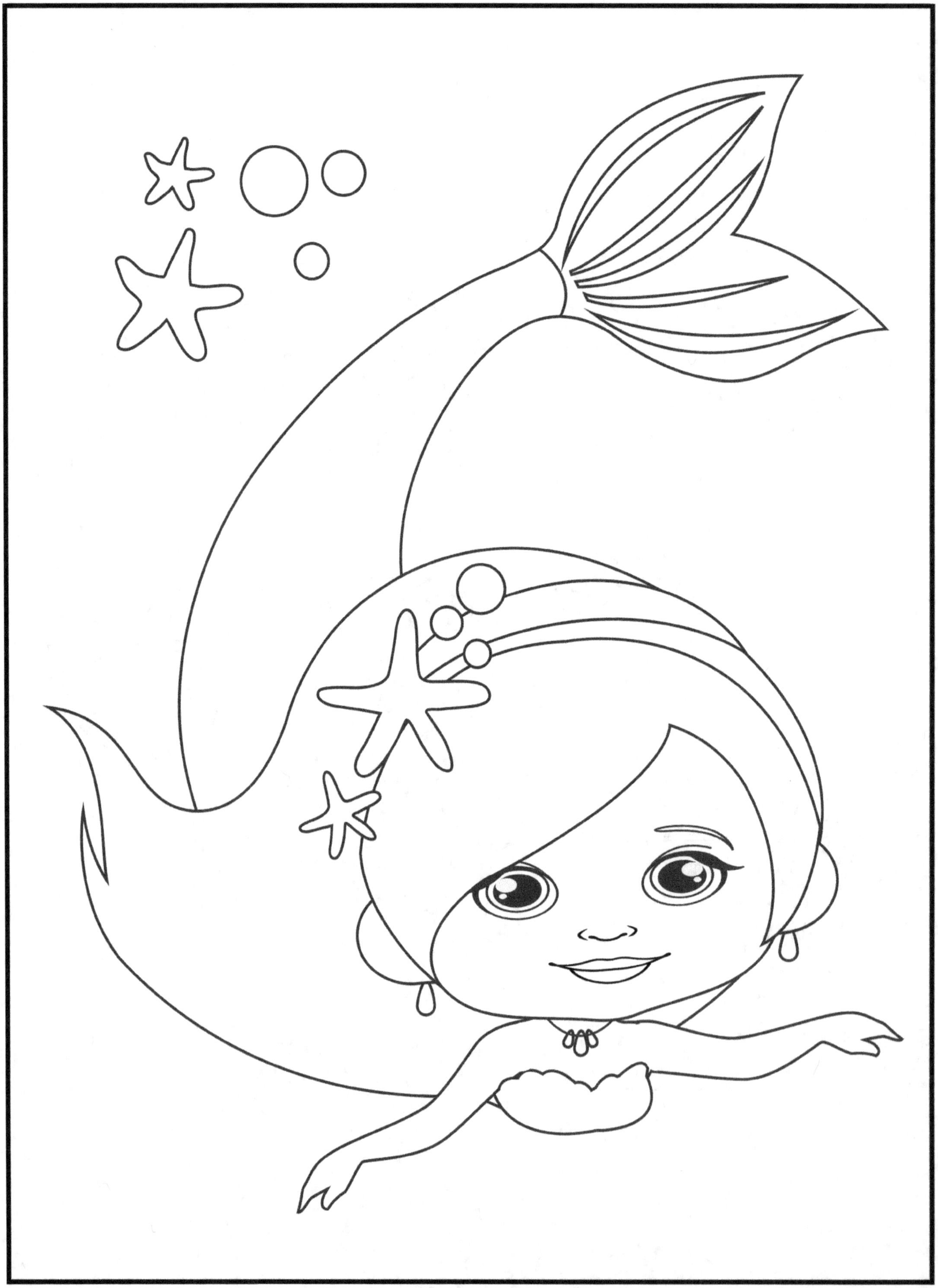

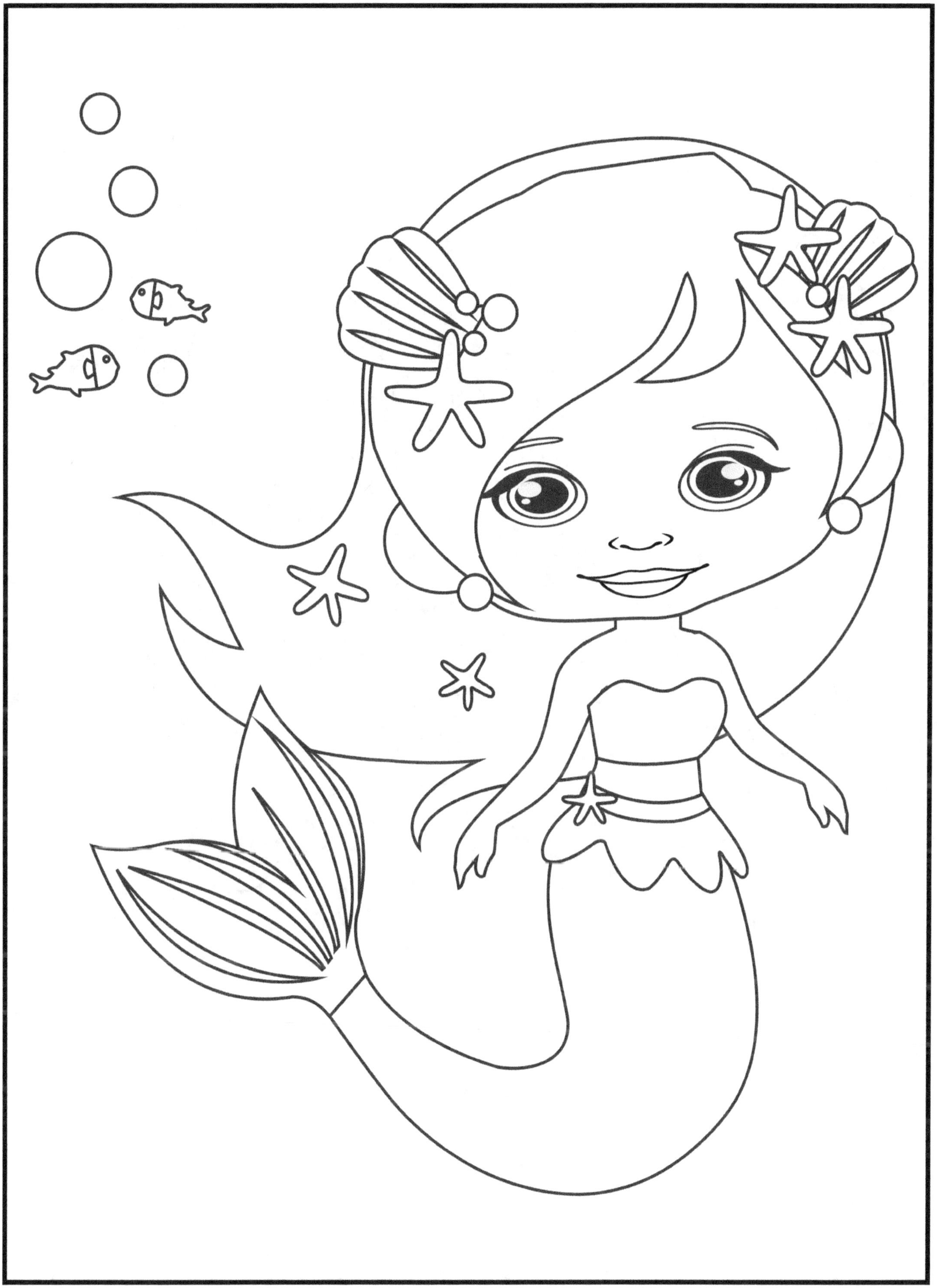

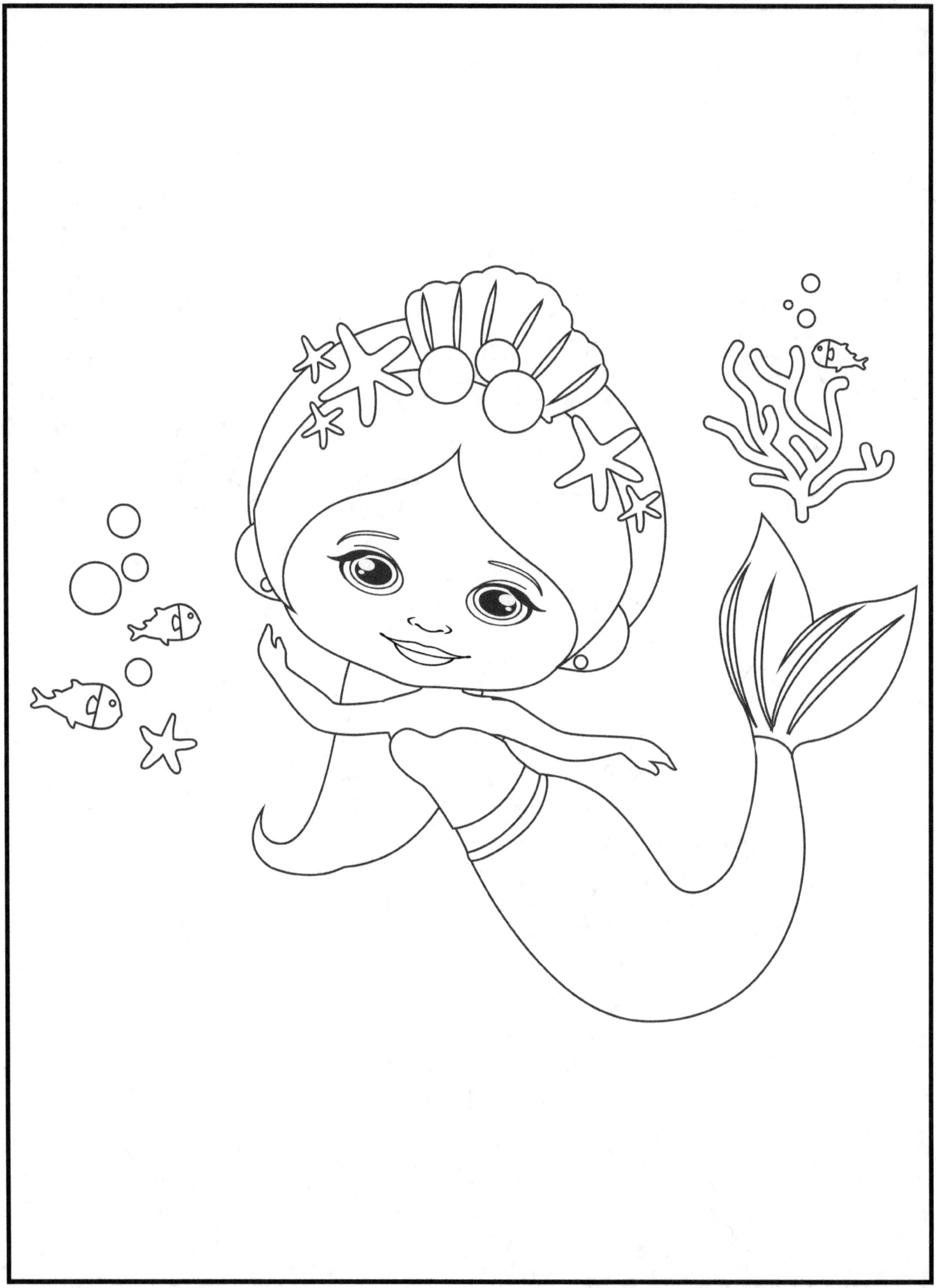

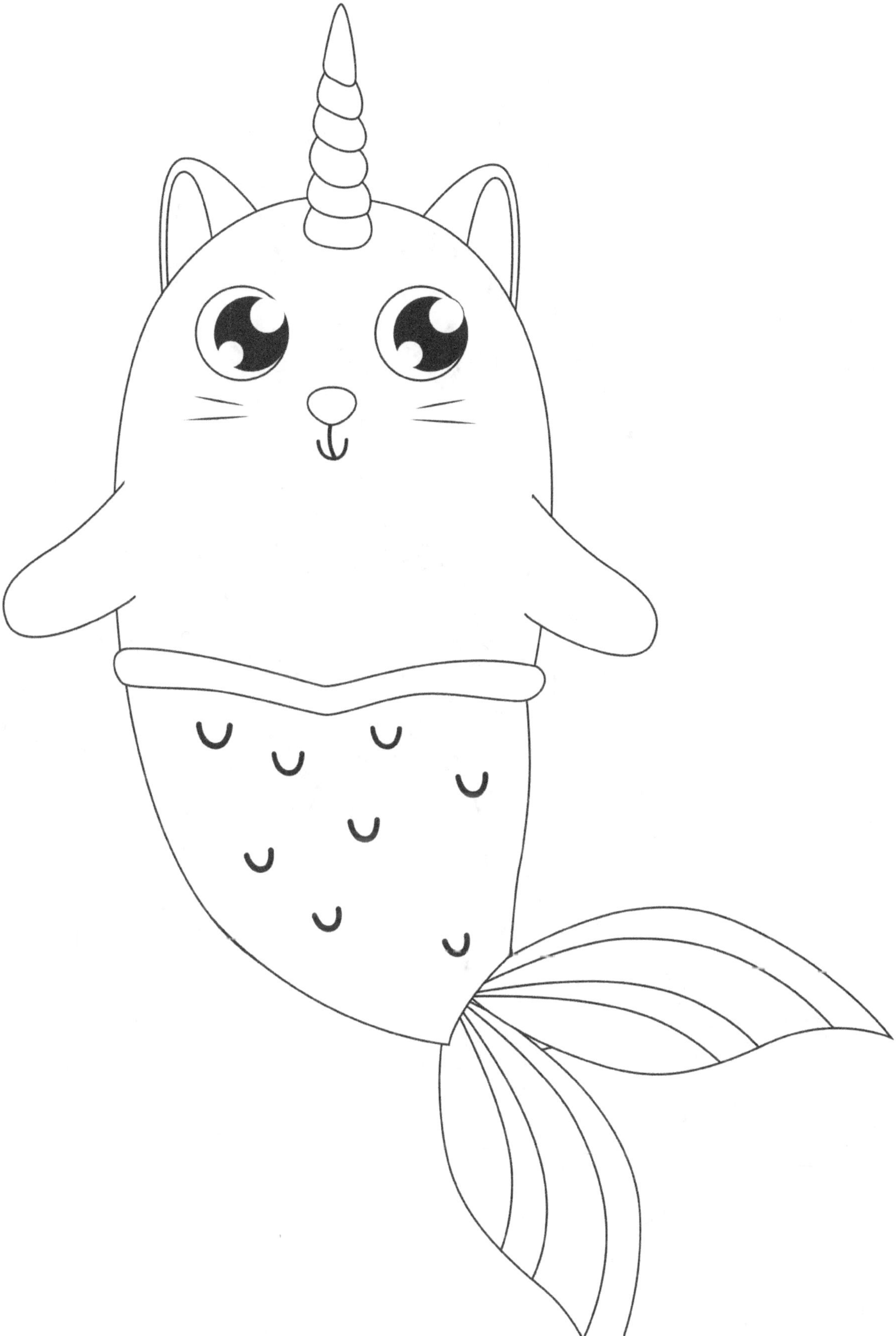

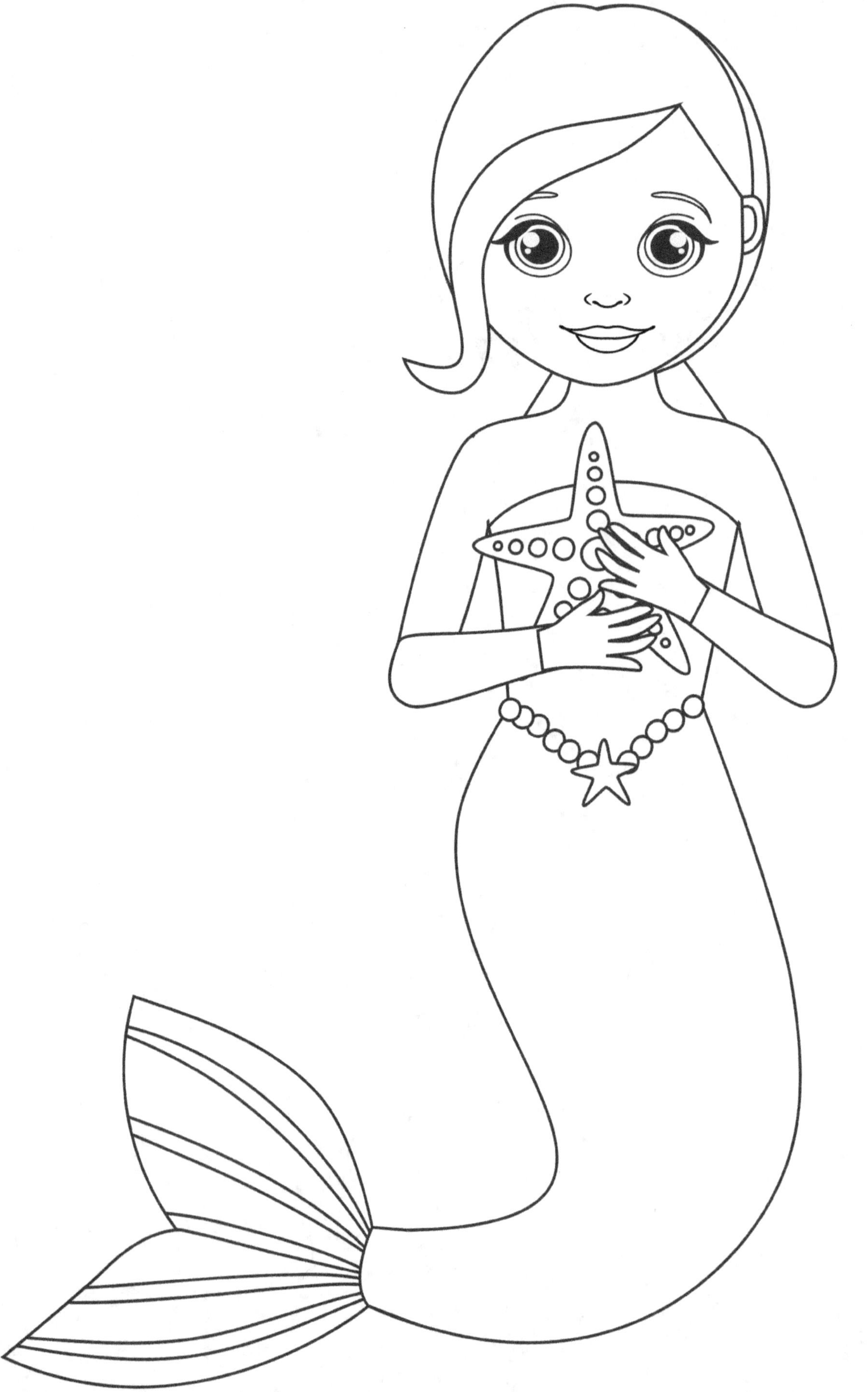

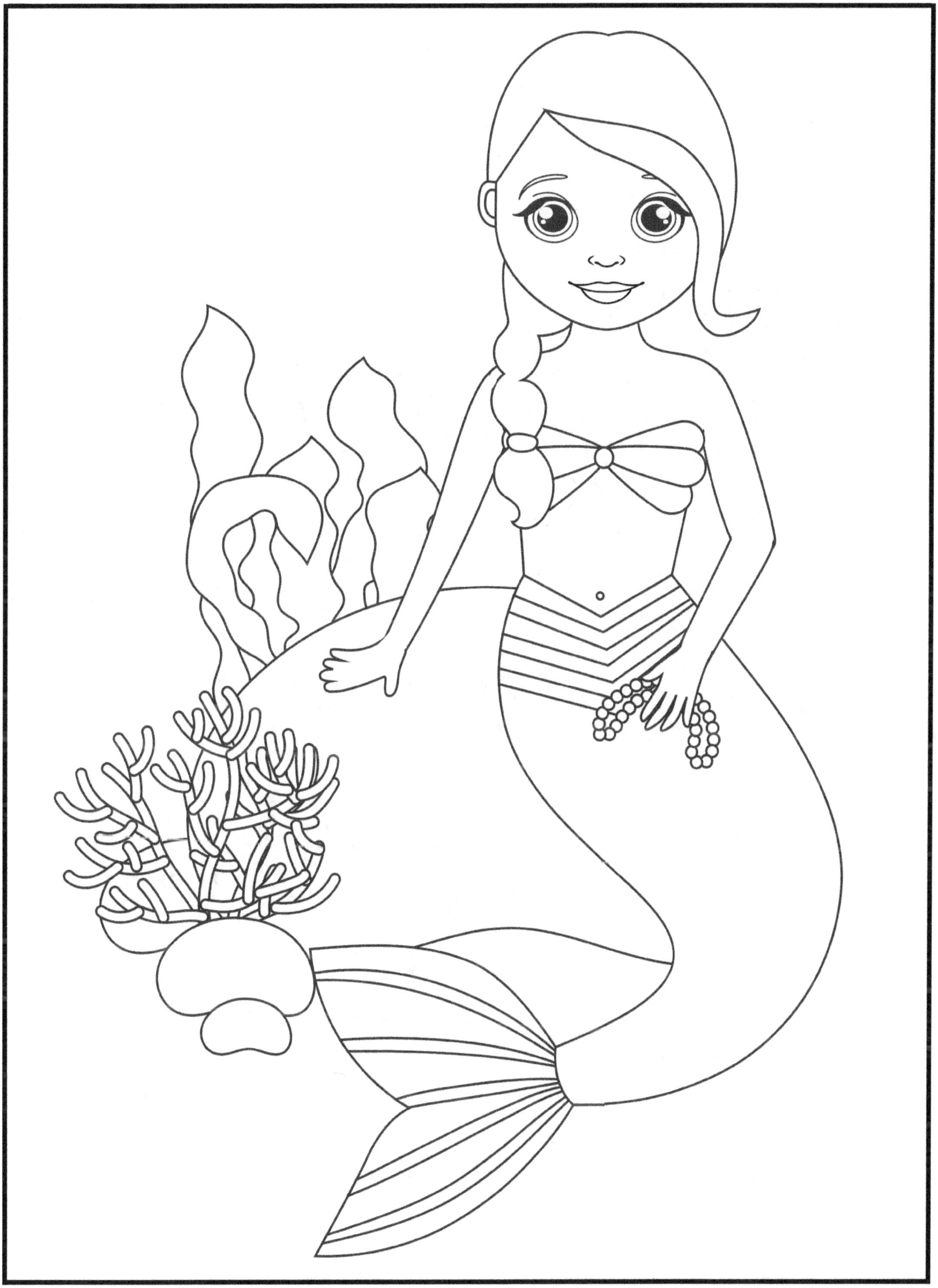

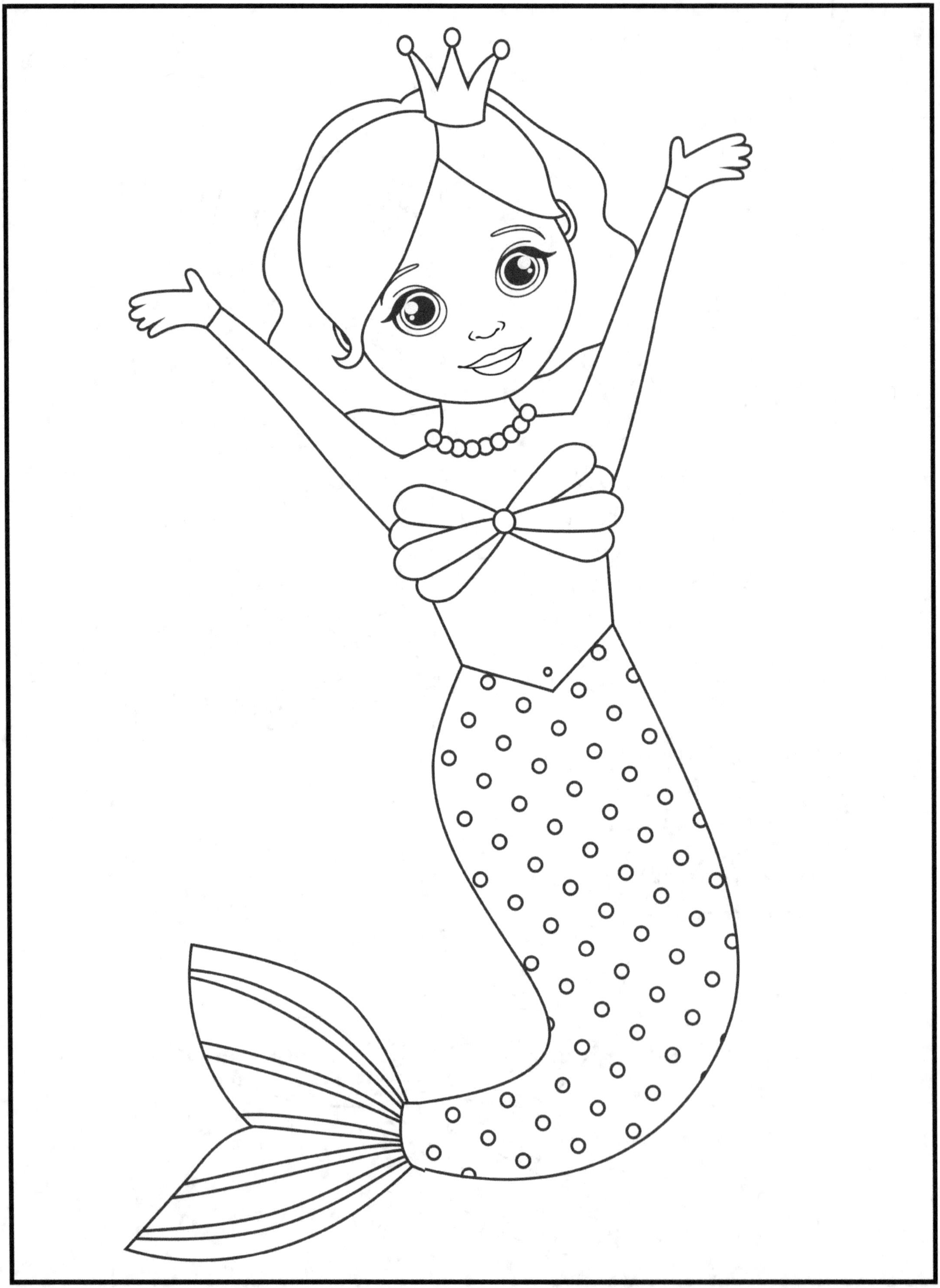

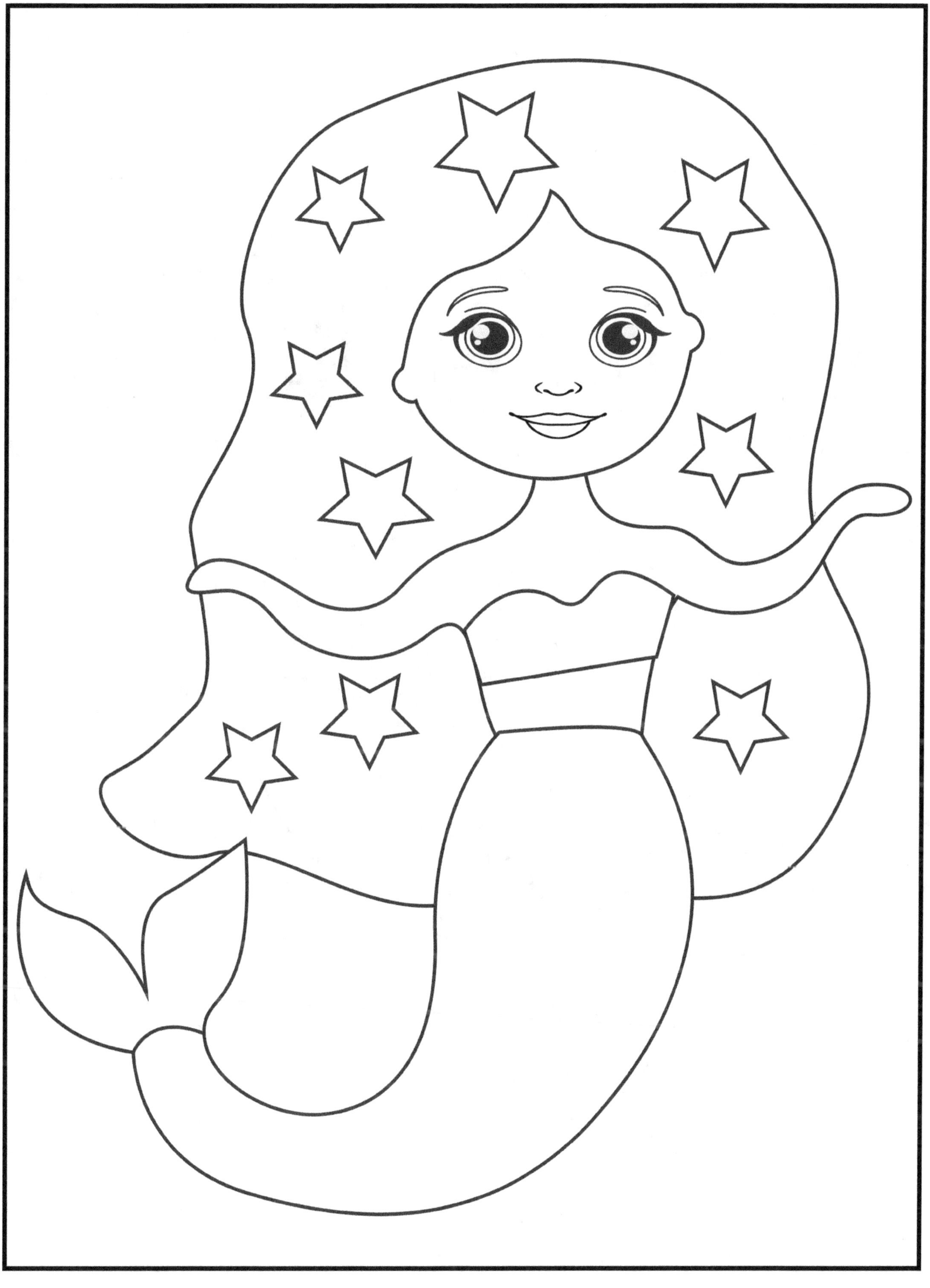

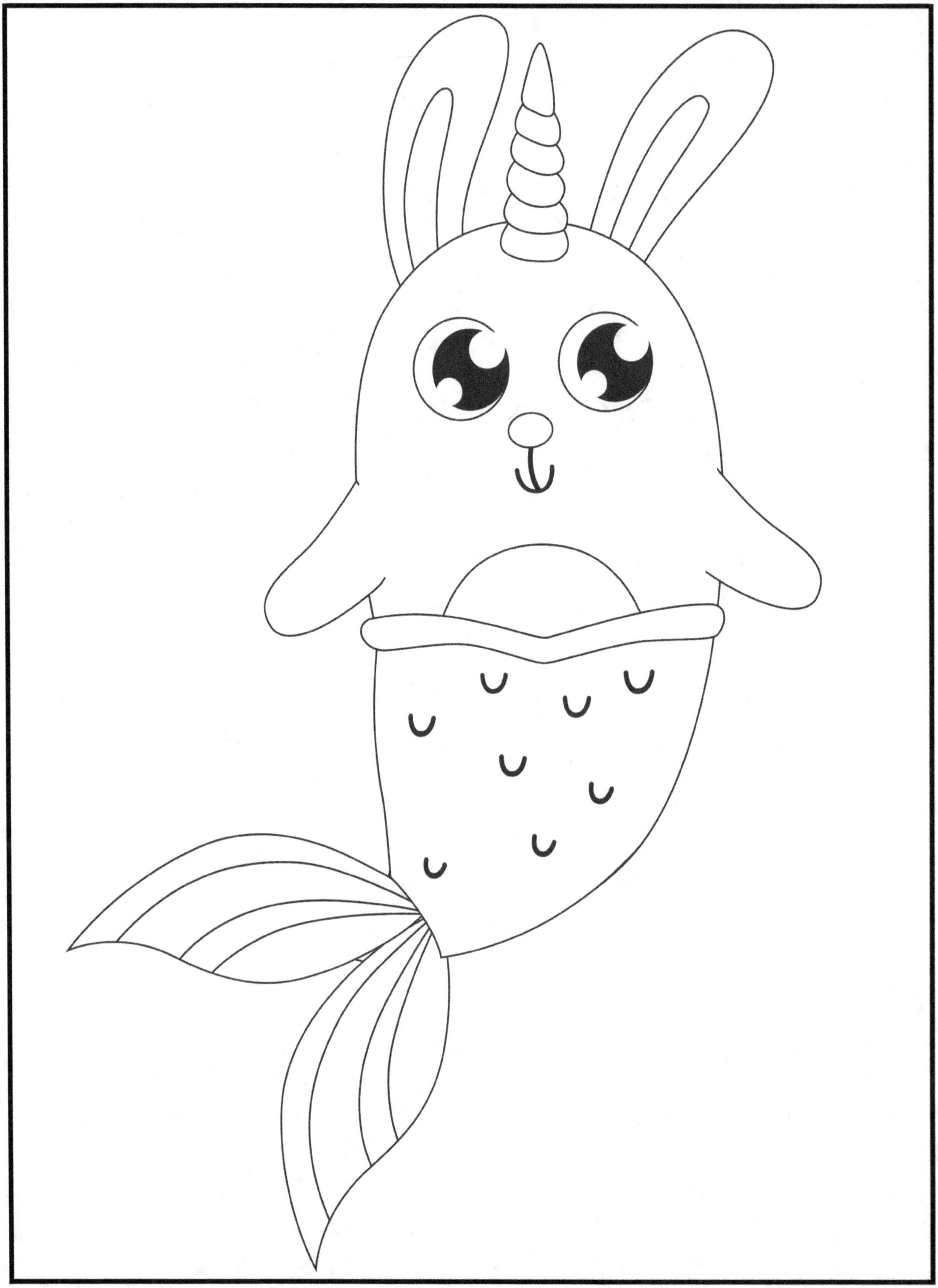

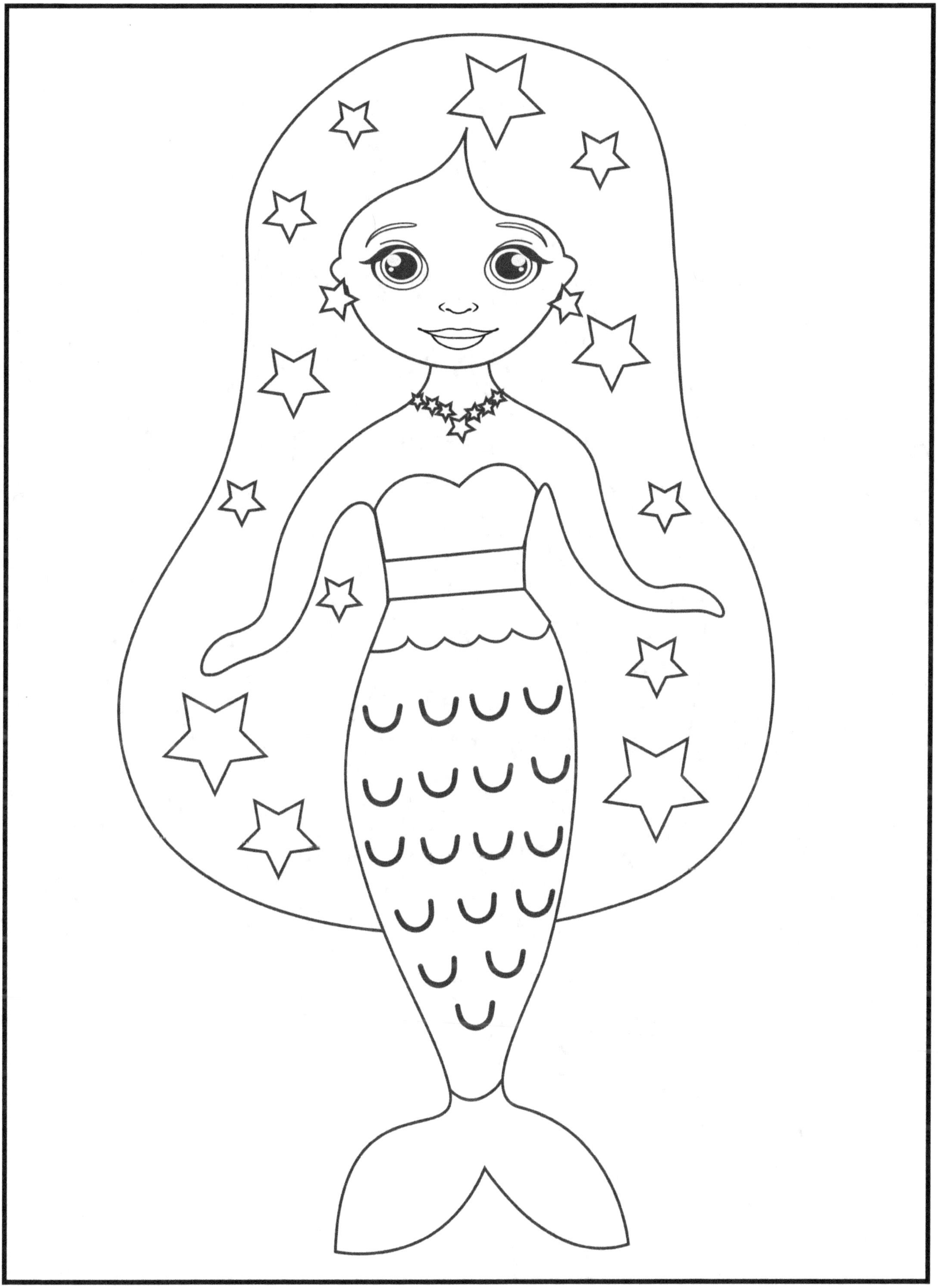

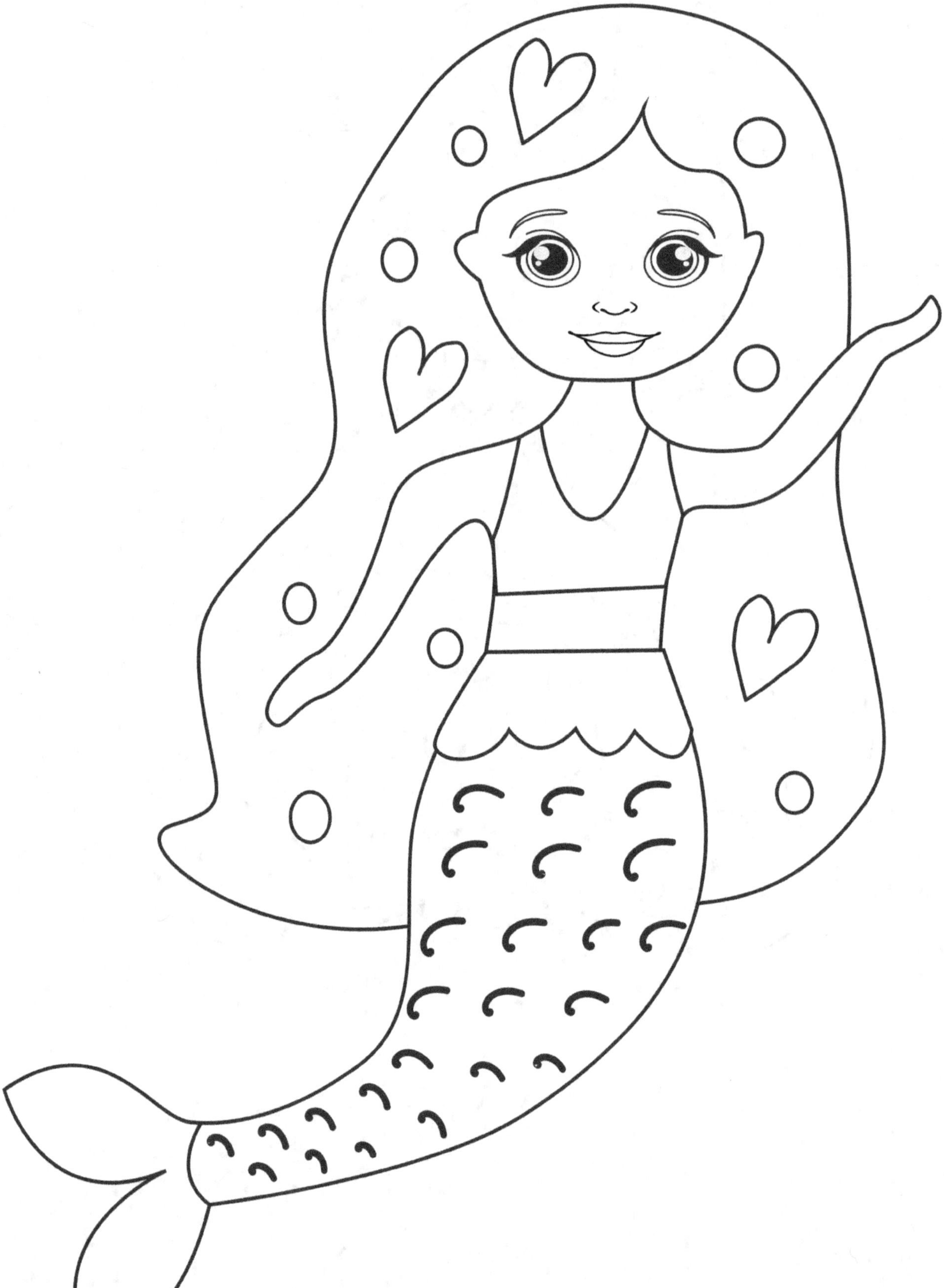

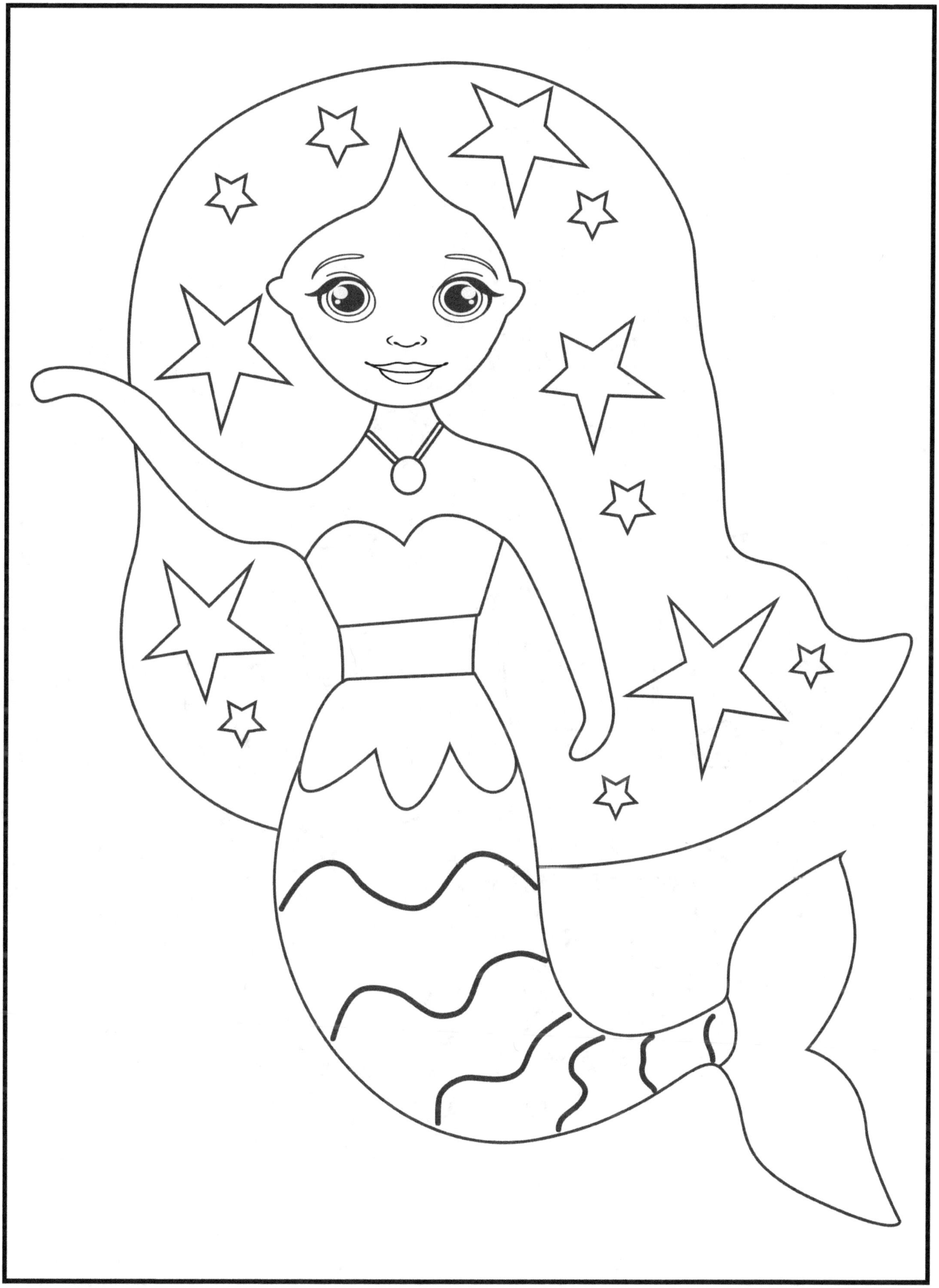

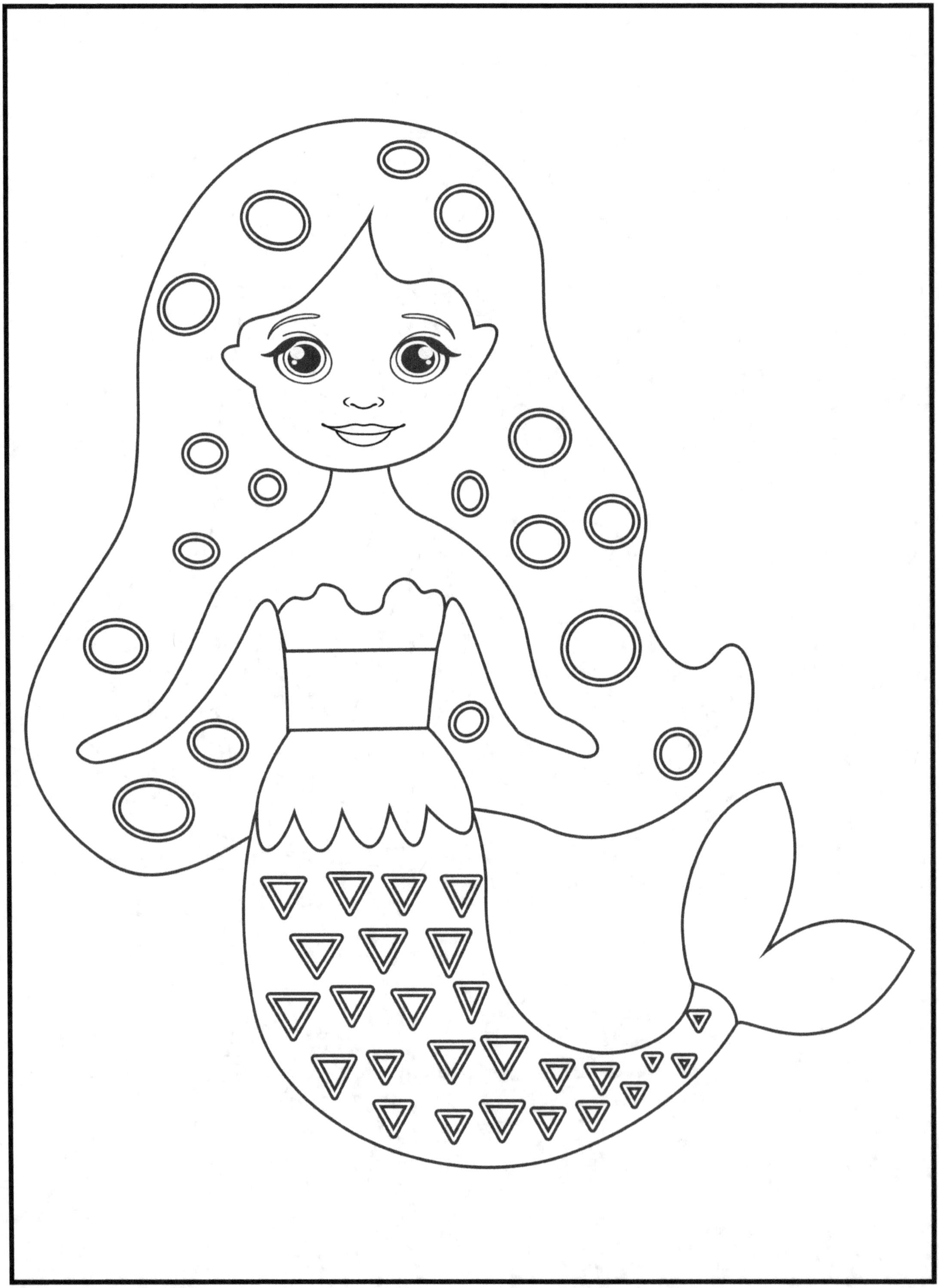

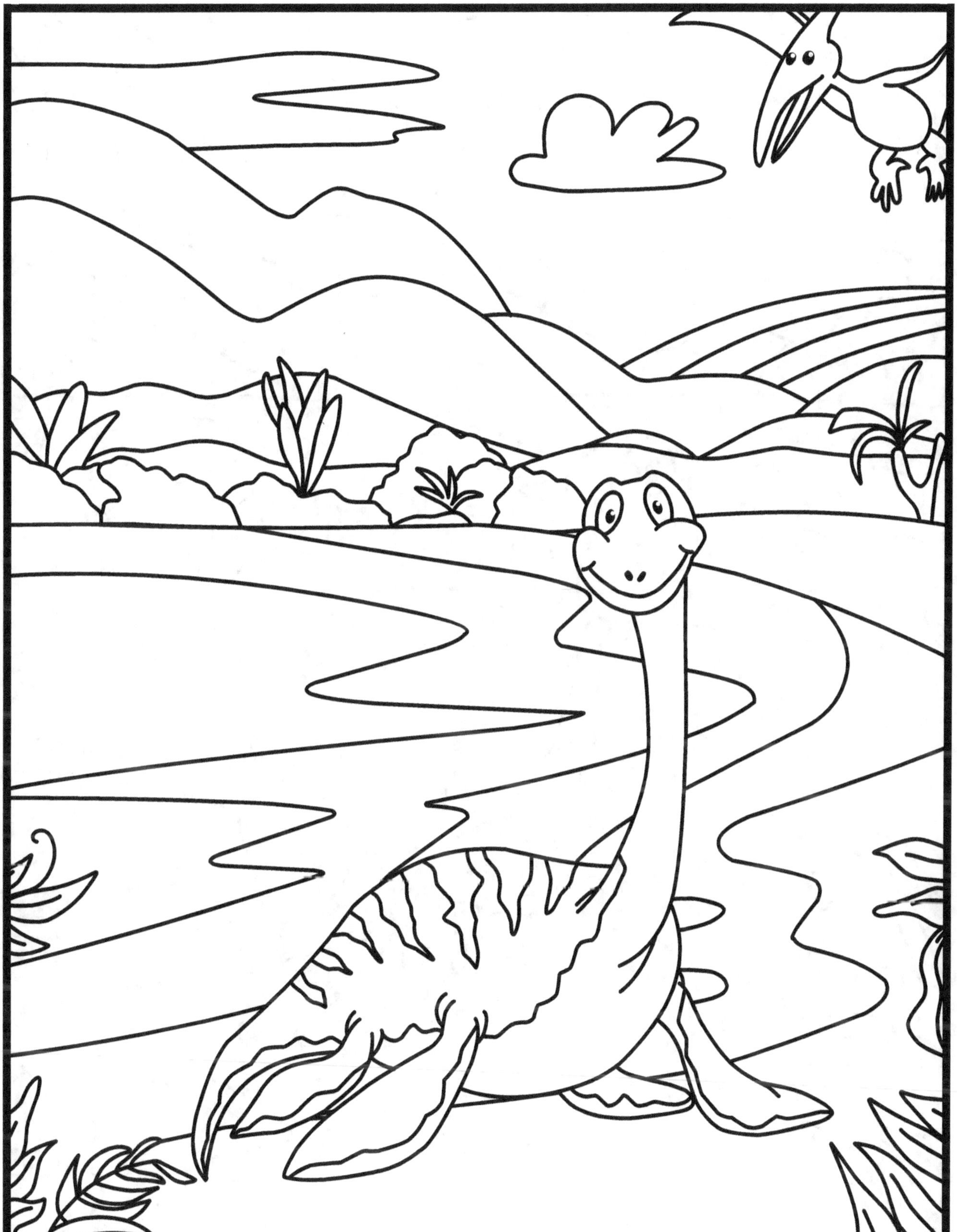

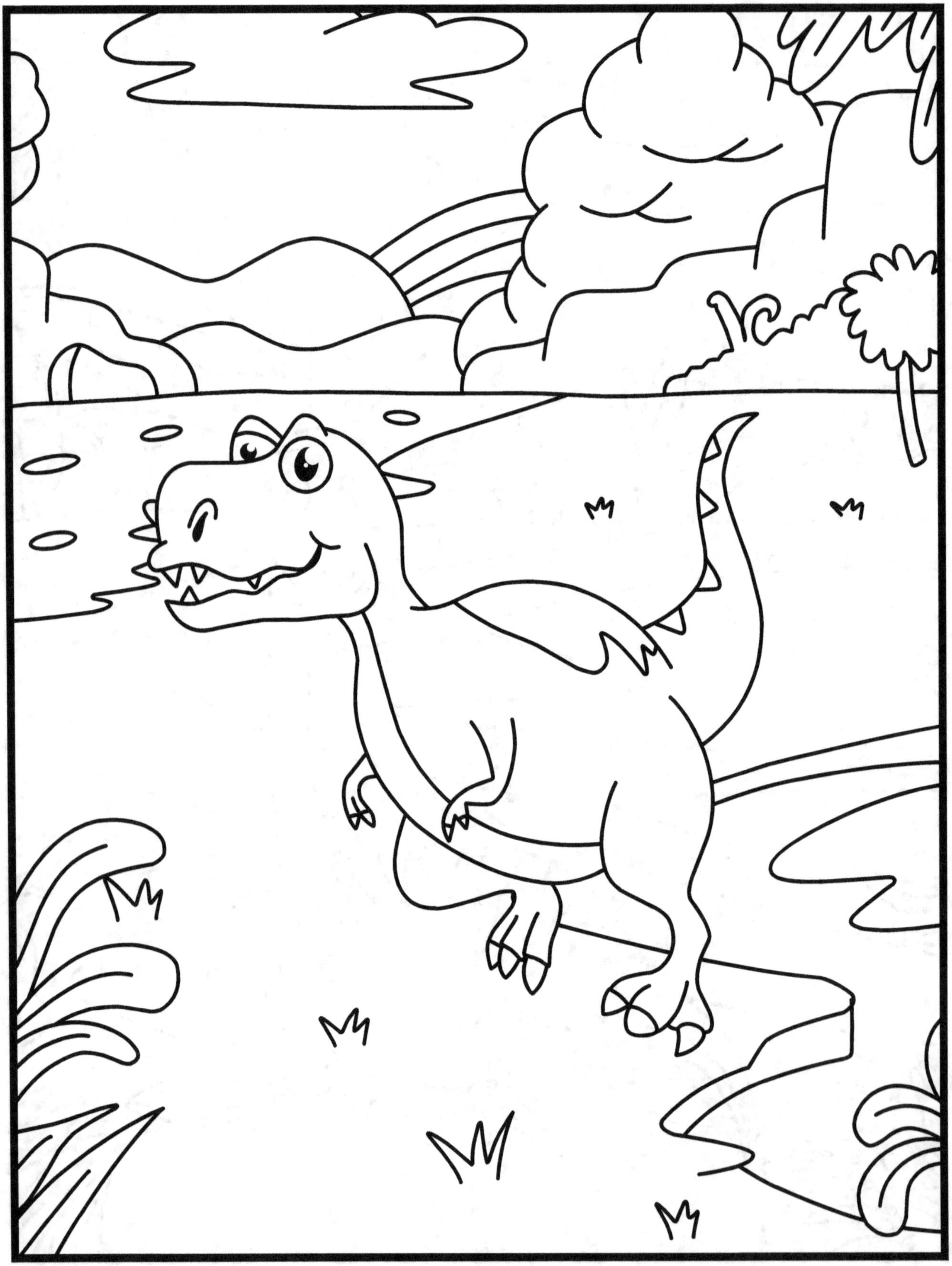

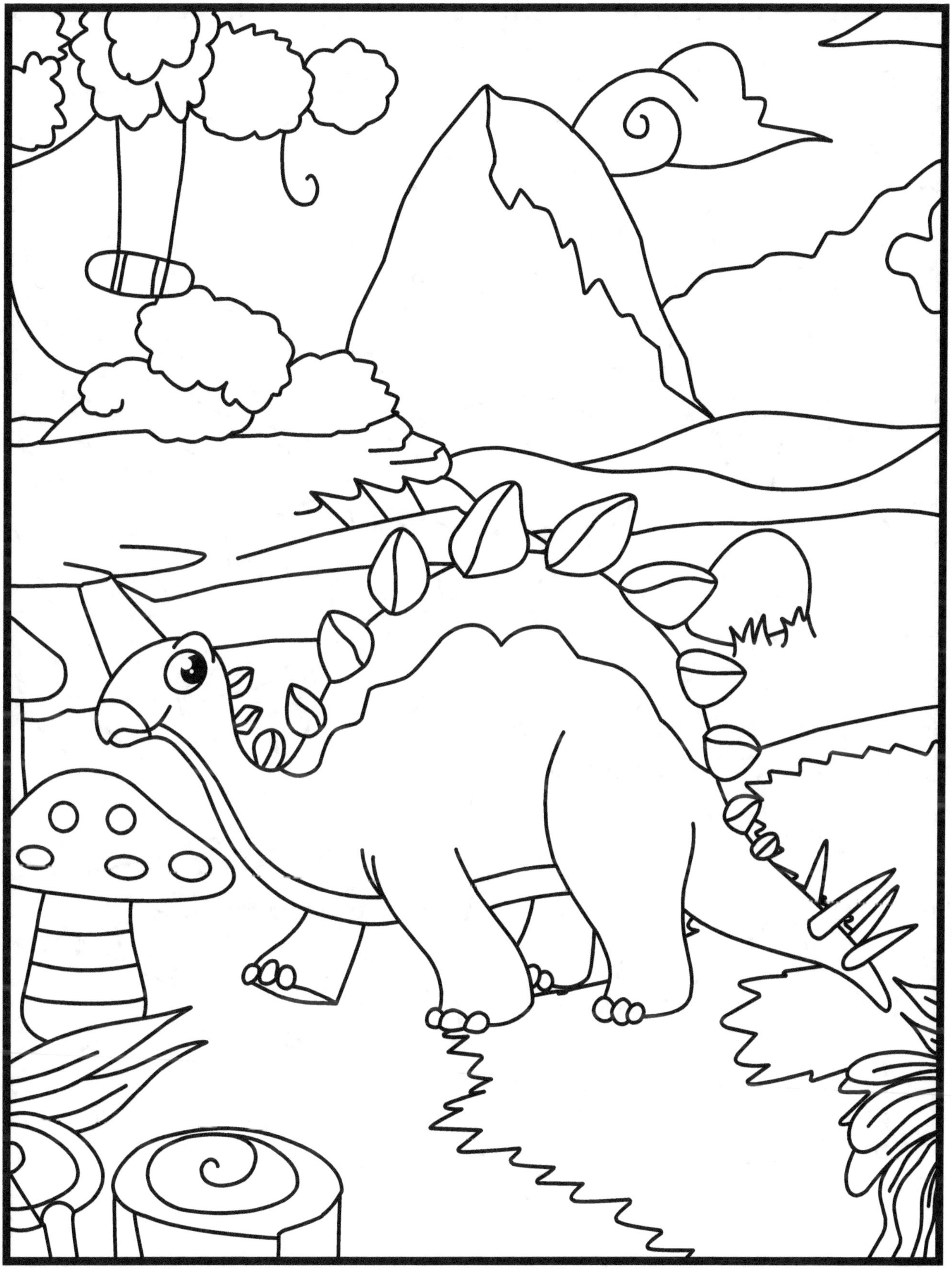

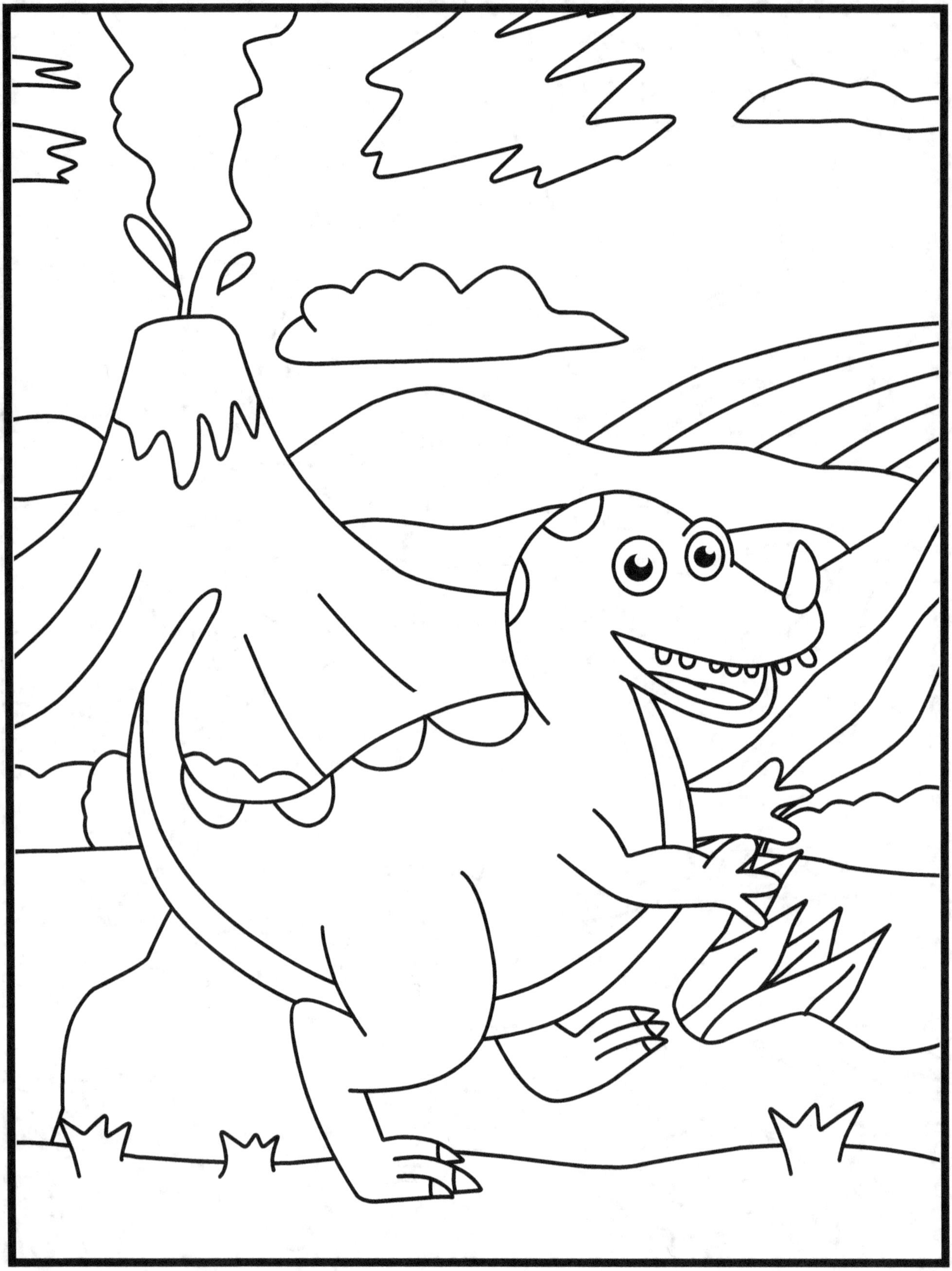

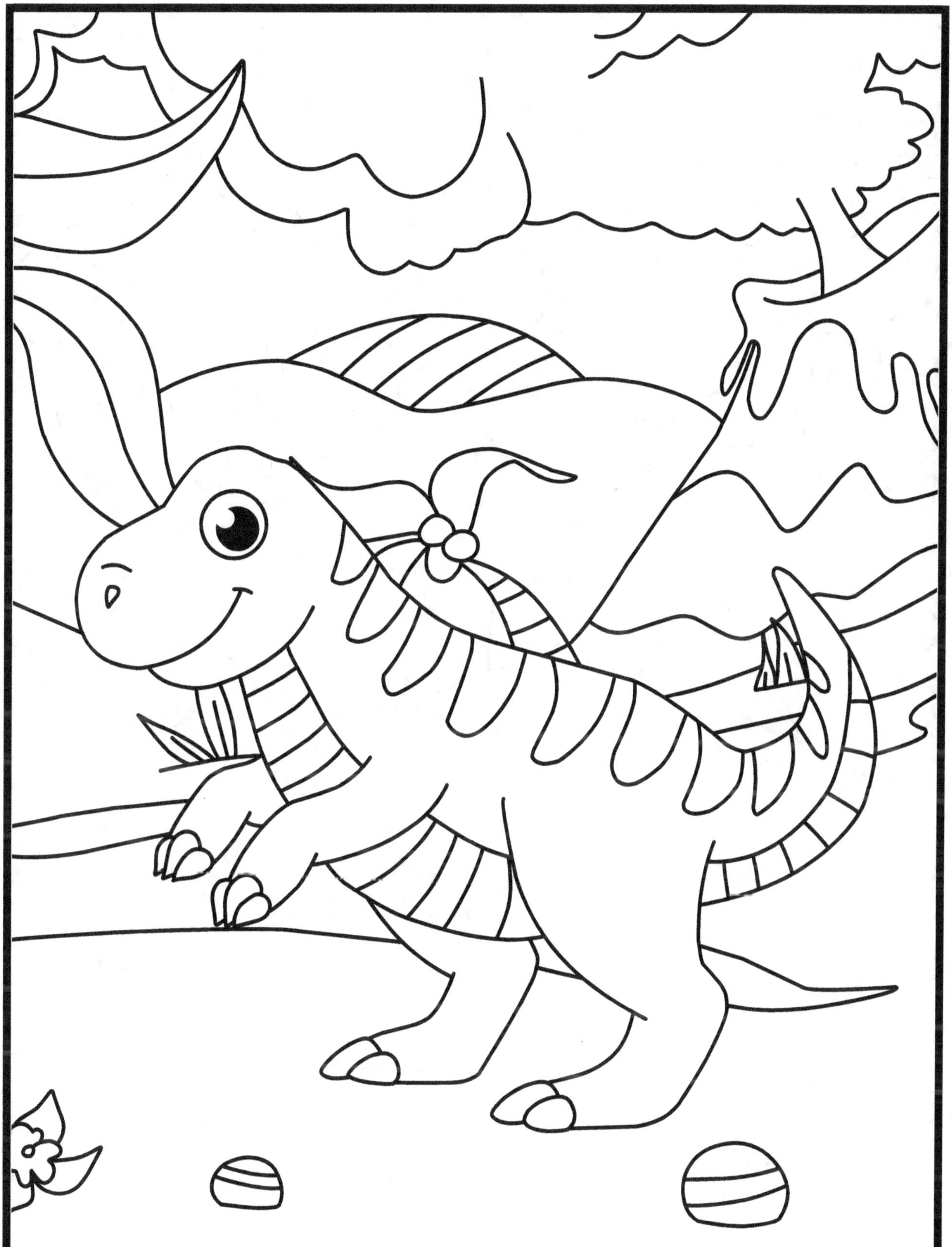

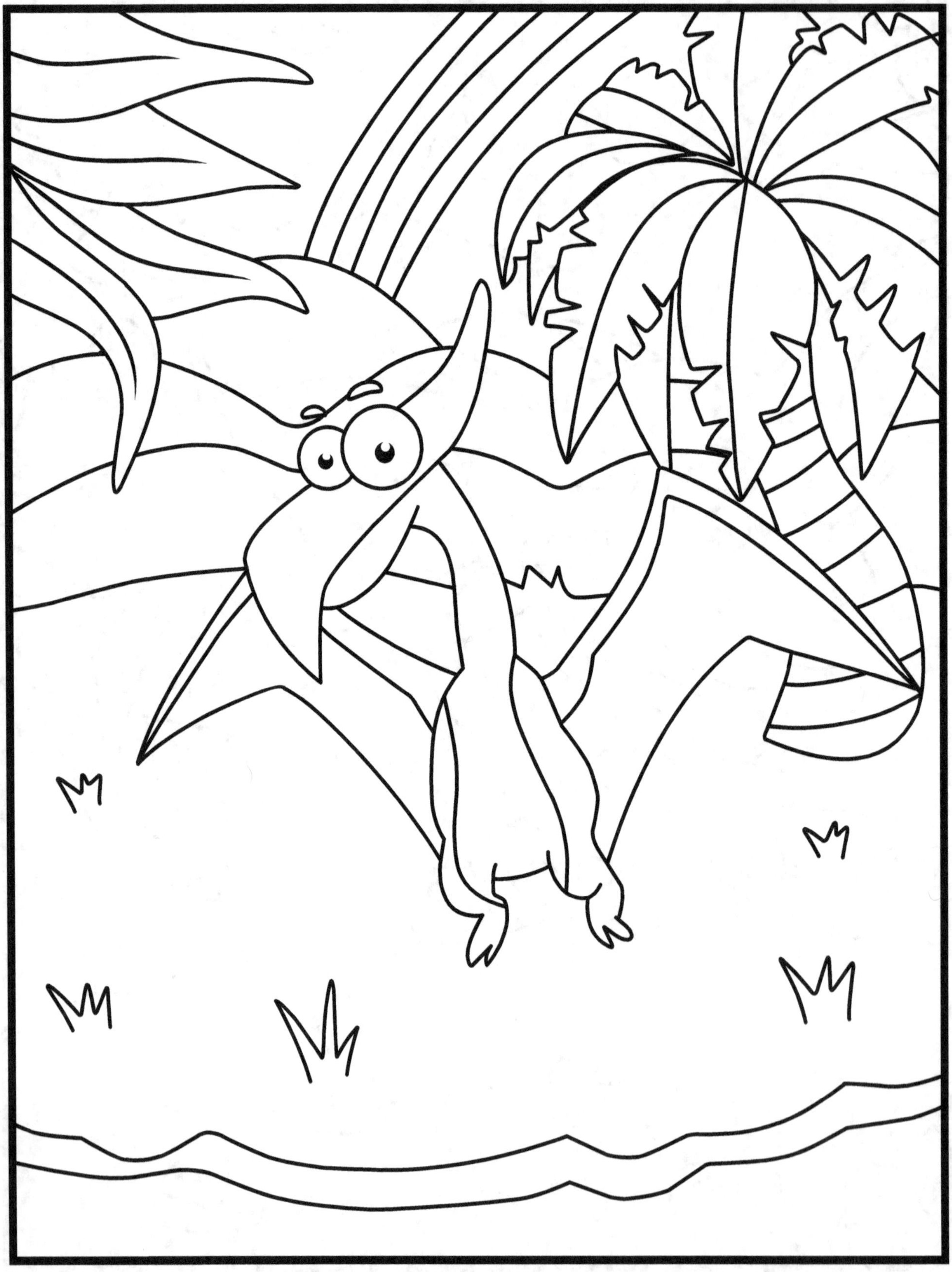

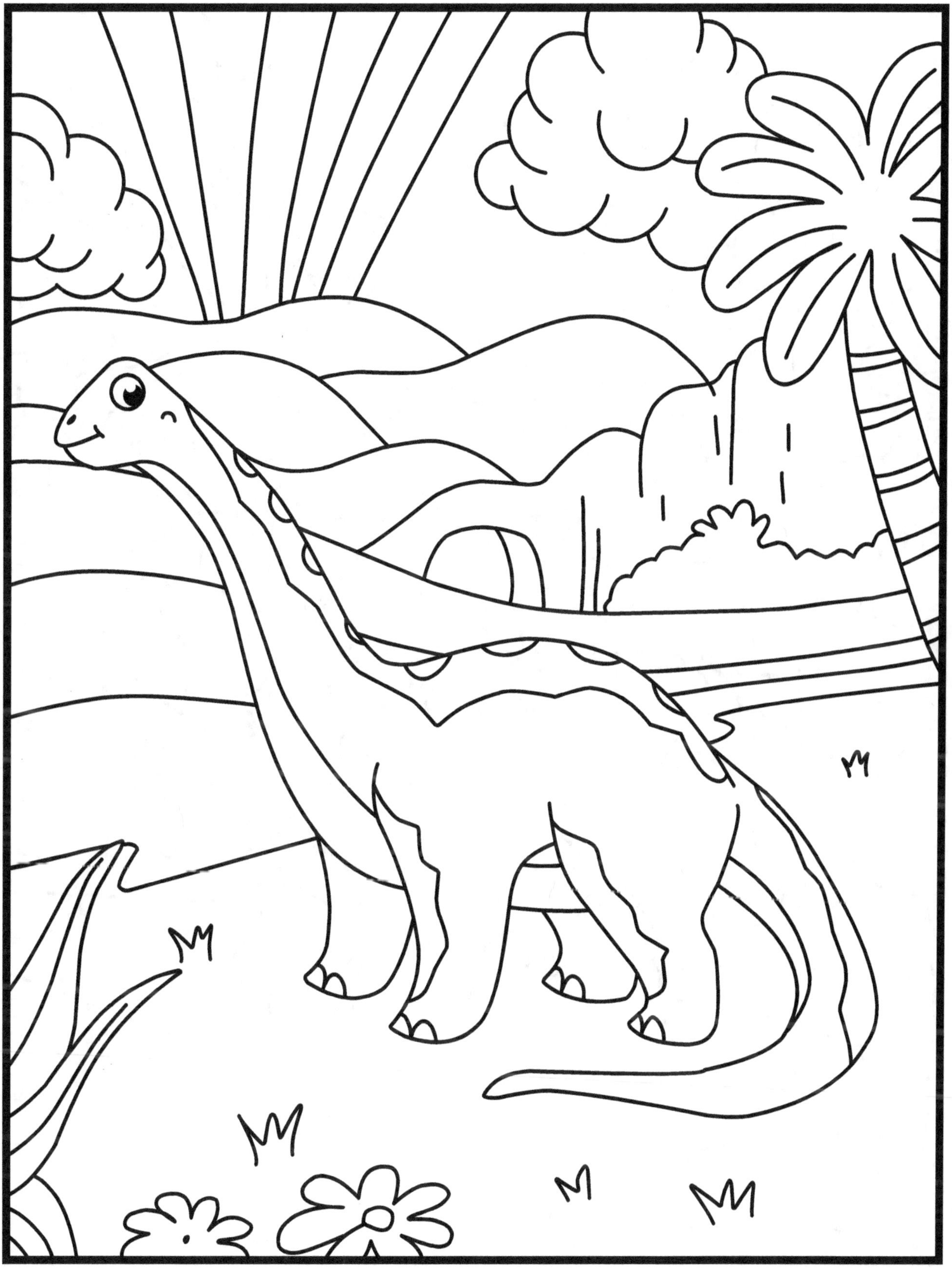

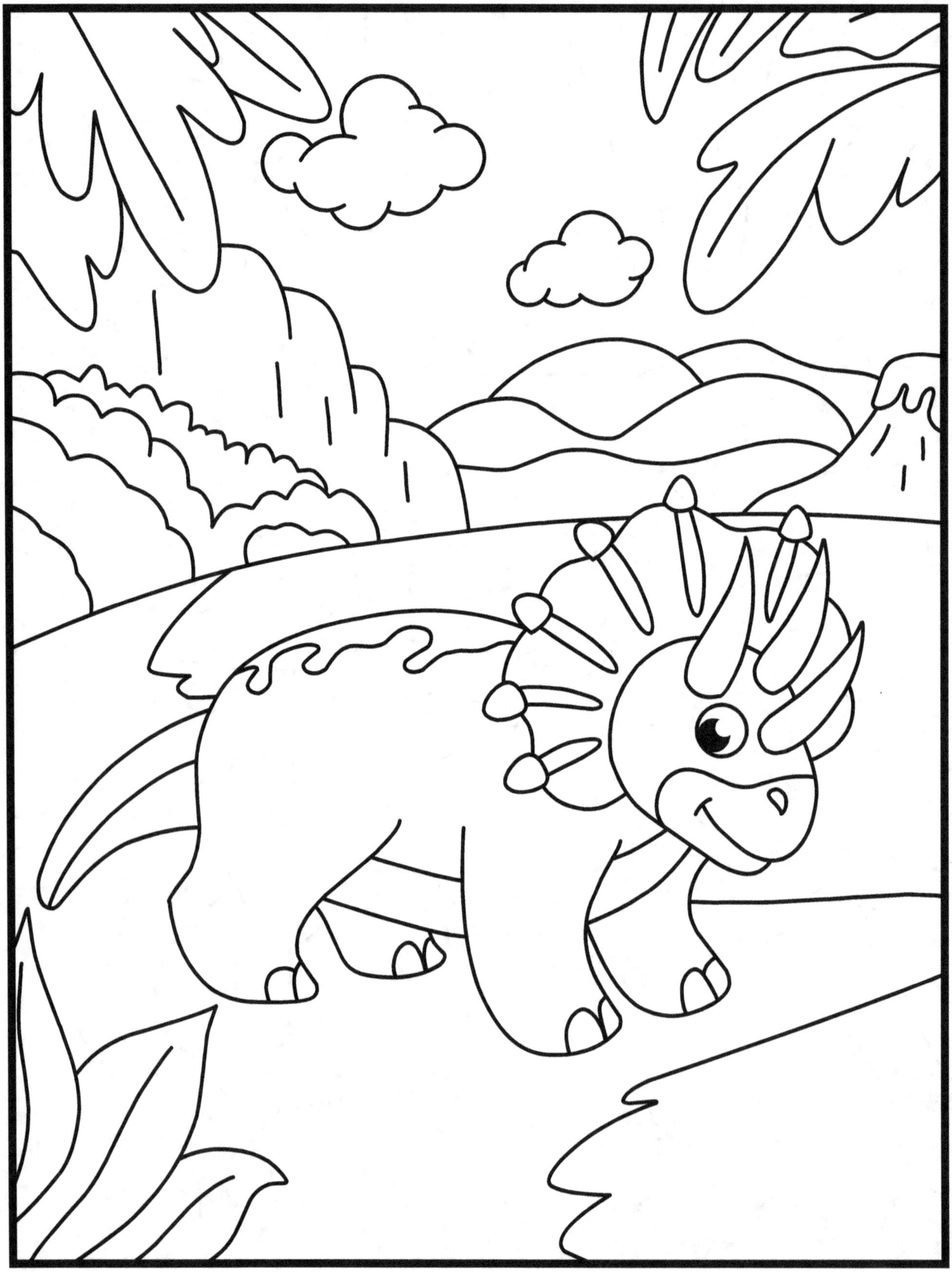

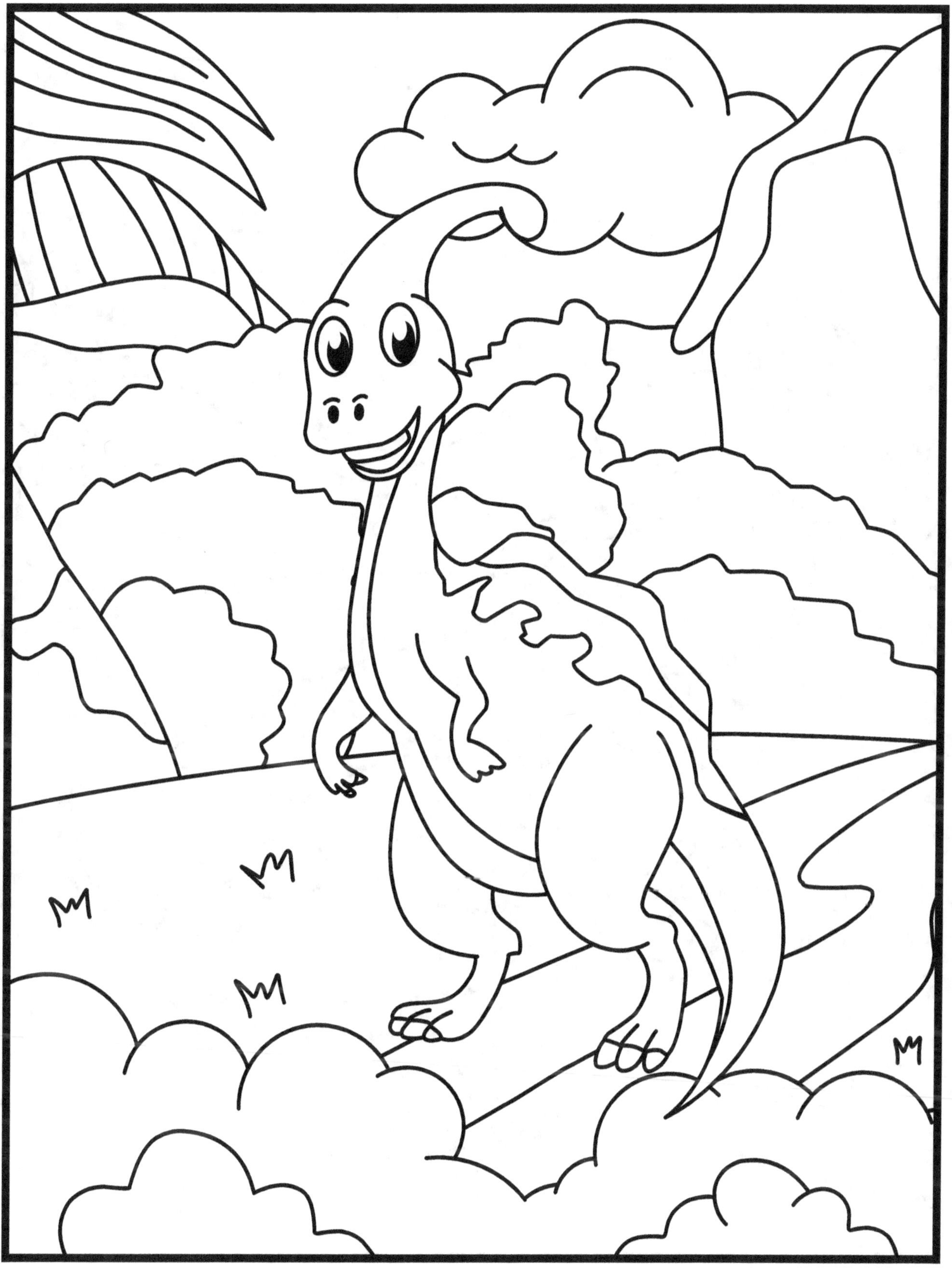

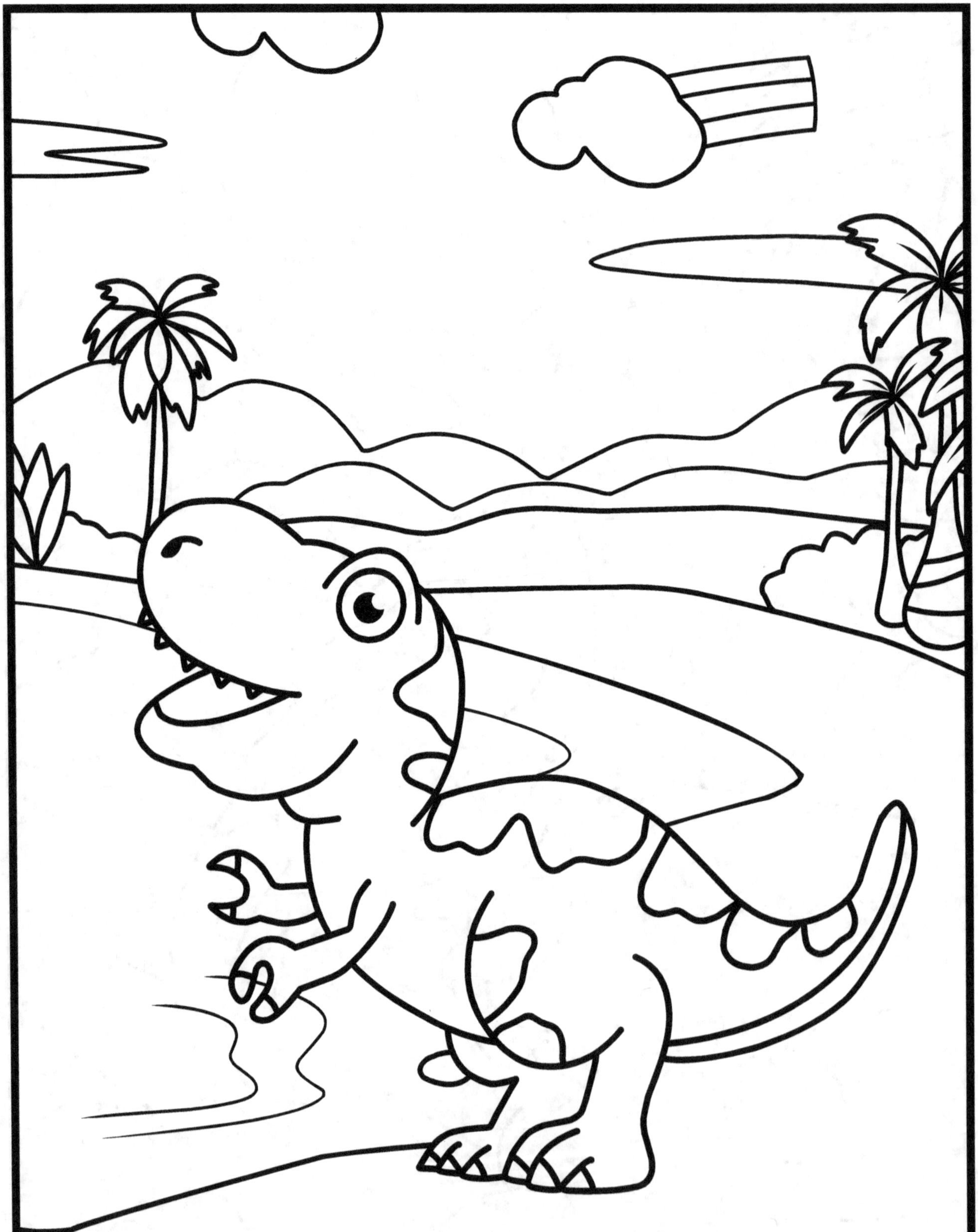

www.ingramcontent.com/pod-product-compliance
Lightning Source LLC
Chambersburg PA
CBHW082220220526
45470CB00010B/3252
* 9 7 9 8 3 2 5 4 9 2 5 8 7 *